VEGETABLES & SALADS

Edited by Norma MacMillan and Wendy James
Home economist Gilly Cubitt

ORBIS PUBLISHING London

Introduction

A vegetable dish or a substantial salad can replace meat,
or make it go further, and is a colourful and satisfying
change from the traditional main course. The recipes here
are economical, healthy and easy to prepare.

Both imperial and metric measures are given for each recipe;
you should follow only one set of measures as they are not
direct conversions. All spoon measures are level unless
otherwise stated. Pastry quantities are based on the amount
of flour used. Dried herbs may be substituted for fresh
herbs; use one-third of the quantity.

Photographs were supplied by Editions Atlas, Editions Atlas/Cedus, Editions
Atlas/Masson, Editions Atlas/Zadora, Flour Advisory Board, Archivio IGDA,
Lavinia Press Agency, Orbis GmbH, Pasta Information Centre, Tate and Lyle
Refineries Ltd.

The material in this book has previously appeared in *The Complete Cook*

First published 1981 in Great Britain by Orbis Publishing Limited,
20–22 Bedfordbury, London WC2

© EDIPEM, Novara 1976
© 1978, 1979, 1980, 1981 Orbis Publishing, London

ISBN 0-85613-375-2
Printed in Singapore

Contents

Crudités with garlic mayonnaise

Overall timing 30 minutes

Freezing Not suitable

To serve 4–6

	Canned mushrooms	
	Canned artichoke hearts	
	Selection of raw vegetables (carrot sticks, radish roses, tomato wedges, chicory leaves)	
	Cooked green beans	
	Gherkins	
	Black olives	
Garlic mayonnaise		
4	Large garlic cloves	4
1	Egg yolk	1
	Salt and pepper	
4 fl oz	Olive oil	120 ml
2 teasp	Hot water	2x5 ml
2 tbsp	Lemon juice	2x15 ml

Drain the mushrooms and artichoke hearts. Quarter the hearts. Arrange all the vegetables on a serving platter with the gherkins and olives, leaving space in the centre for the garlic mayonnaise.

Peel the garlic. Crush in a mortar with a pestle until reduced to a pulp. Add the egg yolk and seasoning and continue mixing with the pestle until smooth and creamy.

Very gradually add the oil, beating well after each addition. Do not hurry this process or you will curdle the mayonnaise. When all the oil has been incorporated and the mixture is thick, beat in the water and lemon juice.

Pour the mayonnaise into a bowl and place in the centre of the vegetables for dipping.

Variation

Almost any combination of vegetables may be served with the mayonnaise.

Stuffed mushrooms

Overall timing 1 hour

Freezing Suitable: reheat in 375°F (190°C) Gas 5 oven for 10 minutes

To serve 4

8	Cup mushrooms	8
2 oz	Fresh breadcrumbs	50 g
¼ pint	Warm milk	150 ml
1	Garlic clove	1
	Salt and pepper	
1	Egg	1
1	Egg yolk	1
4 oz	Grated Parmesan cheese	125 g
2 teasp	Chopped fresh marjoram	2x5 ml
8 teasp	Oil	8x5 ml
	Fresh parsley	

Preheat the oven to 350°F (180°C) Gas 4.

Carefully detach mushroom caps from stalks. Wipe caps and reserve. Chop stalks.

Soak breadcrumbs in warm milk, then squeeze out well, reserving milk. Peel garlic and place in mortar or blender with mushroom stalks, a little of the reserved milk and seasoning. Pound or blend till well combined. Put mixture into a bowl and add egg, egg yolk, grated Parmesan, marjoram and 2 teasp (2x5 ml) of oil. Mix well until creamy, then add salt.

Spread stuffing into hollow of each mushroom cap using a dampened knife. Arrange the stuffed mushrooms in an oiled baking dish. Sprinkle the top with the remaining oil and pepper and bake for about 30 minutes. Garnish with parsley and serve hot.

Cauliflower fritters

Overall timing 25 minutes

Freezing Not suitable

To serve 4

1	Large cauliflower	1
	Salt	
1	Egg	1
1	Egg white	1
2 oz	Plain flour	50 g
4 oz	Dried breadcrumbs	125 g
	Oil for frying	
	Grated Parmesan cheese	
	Chopped parsley	

Trim cauliflower and divide into 25–30 florets. Cook in boiling salted water for 7–10 minutes or till just tender. Drain and allow to cool.

In a bowl, beat together egg, egg white and a pinch of salt till frothy. Dip each floret into flour, then into egg mixture, then roll in breadcrumbs till well coated.

Heat oil to 320°F (160°C). Deep fry cauliflower till golden brown and crisp. Remove cauliflower from pan with a draining spoon and drain on kitchen paper. Serve hot, sprinkled with salt and a little grated Parmesan and chopped parsley mixed together.

Broccoli vinaigrette

Overall timing 20 minutes plus 20 minutes marination

Freezing Not suitable

To serve 6

1 lb	Broccoli	450 g
	Salt and pepper	
10 tbsp	Oil	10x15 ml
1 teasp	Powdered mustard	5 ml
4 tbsp	White wine vinegar	4x15 ml
1 teasp	Brown sugar	5 ml
1	Onion	1
2 tbsp	Chopped chives	2x15 ml
2 tbsp	Chopped parsley	2x15 ml
1 tbsp	Chopped fresh tarragon	15 ml
5	Small gherkins	5
2	Hard-boiled eggs	2
2	Tomatoes	2
5	Radishes	5

Trim broccoli leaves and coarse stems, then cook in boiling salted water for about 10 minutes. Drain well, then chop and divide pieces between six serving dishes or place in salad bowl.

Beat together oil, mustard, vinegar, sugar and seasoning. Peel and finely chop the onion and add to dressing with herbs. Finely chop gherkins and eggs and stir into dressing.

Blanch, peel and finely chop tomatoes. Chop radishes and stir both into dressing. Pour over broccoli and mix well. Leave for 20 minutes until completely cold. Serve with buttered toast.

Pepper salad

Overall timing 30 minutes including cooling

Freezing Not suitable

To serve 4

4	Large red and yellow peppers	4
8 tbsp	Olive oil	8x15 ml
1 oz	Parmesan or strong Cheddar cheese	25 g
1 tbsp	Dried breadcrumbs	15 ml
2 tbsp	Capers	2x15 ml
	Pinch of dried marjoram or mint	
	Sea-salt	
1 tbsp	Vinegar	15 ml

Preheat the grill.

Halve peppers and place, rounded side up, under grill. Cook for a few minutes till skins are charred, then peel. Cut in half again and deseed.

Heat oil in frying pan and fry peppers gently for 7 minutes on each side. Arrange peppers in serving dish, alternating colours to achieve a spoked effect.

Grate cheese. Sprinkle over peppers with breadcrumbs, capers, marjoram or mint and sea-salt. Leave to cool slightly, then pour vinegar over. Serve straight away or cool and serve chilled.

Tuna salad

Overall timing 15 minutes

Freezing Not suitable

To serve 4

1	Bulb of fennel	1
	Salt and pepper	
4	Tomatoes	4
6½ oz	Can of tuna	184 g
3 tbsp	Oil	3 x 15 ml
1 tbsp	Wine vinegar	15 ml
	Chopped parsley	
1 oz	Black olives	25 g

Trim and slice the fennel. Blanch in boiling salted water for 5 minutes. Drain. Slice tomatoes. Drain tuna.

Place tuna in centre of serving dish and arrange fennel and tomato slices around it.

In a bowl, mix together oil, vinegar and seasoning. Pour dressing over salad and sprinkle with chopped parsley. Garnish with black olives and fennel leaves, if available.

Asparagus milanese

Overall timing 30 minutes

Freezing Not suitable

To serve 4

1 lb	Asparagus	450 g
	Salt	
2 oz	Grated Parmesan cheese	50 g
2 oz	Butter	50 g

Cook asparagus in boiling salted water for 15–20 minutes till tender. Drain carefully on a tea-towel or kitchen paper, then place on a warmed serving dish and cool slightly. Sprinkle Parmesan over the asparagus tips.

Melt the butter in a small saucepan over a low heat. When golden brown, pour over the Parmesan. Serve immediately.

Alsace salad

Overall timing 15 minutes

Freezing Not suitable

To serve 6

2	Dessert apples	2
3	Boiled potatoes	3
1	Small cooked beetroot	1
2	Frankfurters	2
1	Onion	1
1	Hard-boiled egg	1
2 teasp	Chopped parsley	2x5 ml
	Sprigs of parsley	
8	Walnuts	8
3 tbsp	Olive oil	3x15 ml
1 tbsp	Wine vinegar	15 ml
1 teasp	Powdered mustard	5 ml
	Salt and pepper	

Peel, core and chop apples. Peel and dice potatoes and beetroot. Slice frankfurters. Peel onion and cut into rings. Shell egg and cut into 6 wedges.

Arrange prepared ingredients in rows in a serving dish and sprinkle with parsley. Garnish with parsley sprigs and walnuts.

To make dressing, mix oil with vinegar, mustard and seasoning. Pour dressing over salad and serve immediately.

Fruity celeriac salad

Overall timing 45 minutes

Freezing Not suitable

To serve 4

8 oz	Celeriac	225 g
2	Apples	2
1	Orange	1
2 tbsp	Lemon juice	2x15 ml
2 oz	Cooked tongue	50 g
Dressing		
3 tbsp	Single cream	3x15 ml
5 tbsp	Plain yogurt	5x15 ml
$\frac{1}{2}$ teasp	Strong made mustard	2.5 ml
	Pinch of sugar	
	Salt and pepper	

Peel celeriac. Peel and core apples. Peel orange and roughly chop flesh. Grate celeriac and apples into a bowl, add orange and sprinkle with lemon juice. Cut tongue into thin strips and add to salad.

To make the dressing, mix together the cream, yogurt, mustard, sugar and seasoning. Add to salad, toss well and chill for 30 minutes before serving.

Tangy avocado salad

Overall timing 15 minutes plus chilling

Freezing Not suitable

To serve 4–6

2	Avocados	2
2	Dill pickles	2
2 oz	Pine nuts	50 g
1	Small onion	1
2 tbsp	Oil	2x15 ml
1 tbsp	Lemon juice	15 ml
	Salt and pepper	
2	Garlic cloves	2
1 tbsp	Chopped fresh mint	15 ml
$\frac{1}{2}$ pint	Plain yogurt	300 ml

Halve avocados and remove stones. Scoop out flesh and dice. Grate or chop pickles. Roughly chop pine nuts. Peel and finely chop onion.

Put prepared ingredients into serving dish and stir in oil, lemon juice and seasoning.

Peel and crush garlic and put into a bowl with mint and yogurt. Beat lightly with a fork. Pour over salad and mix in well. Chill for 1 hour.

Spinach and avocado salad

Overall timing 20 minutes plus cooling

Freezing Not suitable

To serve 6

8 oz	Spinach	225 g
½	Lettuce	½
1	Avocado	1
1 tbsp	Oil	15 ml
1 tbsp	Lemon juice	15 ml
	Salt and pepper	
4 tbsp	Thick mayonnaise	4x15 ml
1	Hard-boiled egg	1

Trim spinach and wash thoroughly. Put into a pan with no extra water, cover and cook for 8–10 minutes till tender. Turn into a colander and press with wooden spoon to remove excess liquid. Leave to cool.

Wash, trim and dry lettuce. Reserve six medium-size leaves and finely shred the rest. Cut avocado in half and remove stone. Scoop out flesh and chop finely. Place in bowl with cooled spinach, shredded lettuce, oil and lemon juice. Mix together well and season to taste.

Arrange reserved lettuce leaves on serving plate and divide spinach mixture between them. Pipe or spoon mayonnaise on top. Cut hard-boiled egg into wedges and use to garnish.

Salade niçoise

Overall timing 25 minutes

Freezing Not suitable

To serve 4

1 lb	Waxy potatoes	450 g
	Salt and pepper	
8 oz	Green beans	225 g
4 oz	Large black olives	125 g
2 tbsp	Drained capers	2x15 ml
1	Garlic clove	1
4 tbsp	Olive oil	4x15 ml
1 tbsp	Tarragon vinegar	15 ml
1 teasp	Lemon juice	5 ml
1 tbsp	Chopped parsley	15 ml
1	Large firm tomato	1
6	Anchovy fillets	6

Peel and dice the potatoes. Cook in boiling salted water for about 5 minutes till just tender. Top, tail and string the beans and cut into 1 inch (2.5 cm) lengths. Cook in another pan of boiling salted water for 5 minutes till tender.

Drain the vegetables and rinse under cold water. Drain thoroughly and put into a salad bowl. Add half the olives and the capers.

Peel and crush the garlic clove into a bowl. Add the oil, vinegar, lemon juice, parsley and pepper to taste and mix well, then pour over vegetables. Toss lightly till evenly coated.

Cut the tomato into thin wedges. Arrange on the salad with the remaining olives. Cut the anchovies into strips and arrange in a lattice on top of the salad. Serve immediately with French bread.

Sweet-sour beans

Overall timing 2½ hours plus 2 hours soaking

Freezing Not suitable

To serve 4

8 oz	Dried haricot beans	225 g
1 teasp	Salt	5 ml
1	Carrot	1
1	Onion	1
8	Green olives	8
Dressing		
6 tbsp	Oil	6x15 ml
2 tbsp	Wine vinegar	2x15 ml
1 teasp	Soft brown sugar	5 ml
½ teasp	Ground cinnamon	2.5 ml
	Salt and pepper	
1	Garlic clove	1
1 teasp	Dried savory	5 ml

Put the beans in a saucepan, cover with boiling water and leave to soak for 2 hours.

Add the salt, bring to the boil, cover and simmer for 2–2½ hours or till tender. Drain beans and cool.

Peel and slice carrot. Peel and chop onion. Place in bowl and add beans and olives.

To make dressing, mix all ingredients together. Pour over beans and toss.

Chicory and anchovy salad

Overall timing 15 minutes

Freezing Not suitable

To serve 4

4	Heads of chicory	4
4	Anchovy fillets	4
2 tbsp	Lemon juice	2x15 ml
½ teasp	Salt	2.5 ml
2 tbsp	Chopped parsley	2x15 ml
2	Hard-boiled egg yolks	2
Dressing		
1 tbsp	Wine or cider vinegar	15 ml
1 teasp	French mustard	5 ml
	Salt and pepper	
3 tbsp	Oil	3x15 ml

Trim and chop chicory. Drain and chop anchovy fillets. Place both in salad bowl. Add lemon juice and salt.

To make the dressing, mix together vinegar, mustard and seasoning in a small bowl. Gradually beat in oil until the dressing thickens.

Pour dressing over salad and toss. Sprinkle with chopped parsley and sieved or crumbled egg yolks.

Broccoli with ham

Overall timing 20 minutes

Freezing Not suitable

To serve 4

1¾ lb	Calabrese broccoli	750 g
	Salt and pepper	
2	Onions	2
2 oz	Butter *or*	50 g
3 tbsp	Olive oil	3 x 15 ml
8 oz	Cooked ham	225 g
	Grated nutmeg	

Trim leaves from broccoli and remove coarse stems. Divide into spears. Cook in boiling salted water for 8 minutes. Drain and place in warmed serving dish. Keep hot.

Peel and chop the onions. Heat butter or oil in frying pan and fry onions till transparent. Chop the ham into squares. Add to pan with pepper and nutmeg and cook for 4–5 minutes.

Place ham mixture on top of broccoli and serve immediately.

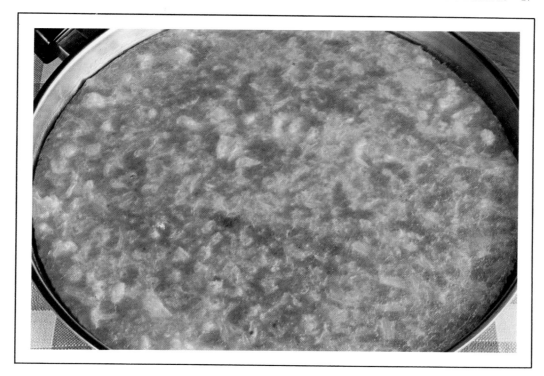

Italian cauliflower omelette

Overall timing 20 minutes

Freezing Not suitable

To serve 2

12 oz	Cauliflower	350 g
	Salt and pepper	
1	Onion	1
2 oz	Butter	50 g
6	Eggs	6
2 tbsp	Grated Parmesan cheese	2x15 ml
½ teasp	Grated nutmeg	2.5 ml

Preheat the grill.

Cut cauliflower into tiny florets and cook in boiling salted water for 3–5 minutes till just tender.

Meanwhile, peel and finely chop onion. Melt butter in a frying pan and fry onion till golden. Add the drained cauliflower and seasoning and cook for 2 minutes, spreading evenly in the pan.

Beat the eggs in a bowl with the Parmesan and nutmeg. Pour evenly over the cauliflower and cook over a moderate heat till the omelette is nearly set.

Put the frying pan under the grill and cook till the top of the omelette is golden. Slide omelette on to a warmed serving plate and cut in two to serve.

Aubergine cheese bake

Overall timing 2¼ hours

Freezing Suitable: bake from frozen in 350°F (180°C) Gas 4 oven for 45 minutes

To serve 4

1¼ lb	Aubergines	600 g
	Salt and pepper	
2 tbsp	Plain flour	2x15 ml
	Oil	
1	Small onion	1
14 oz	Can of tomatoes	397 g
½ teasp	Dried basil	2.5 ml
8 oz	Mozzarella cheese	225 g
3 oz	Grated Parmesan cheese	75 g

Remove stalks from aubergines and cut lengthways into ½ inch (12.5 mm) thick slices. Sprinkle with salt. Leave for 1 hour, then rinse and pat dry. Coat with flour.

Preheat the oven to 350°F (180°C) Gas 4.

Heat oil in a large frying pan and fry aubergine slices on both sides till golden. Drain on kitchen paper and keep warm.

Peel and finely chop onion. Fry till transparent, adding more oil to pan if necessary. Mash tomatoes and juice and add to pan with seasoning. Cook for 10 minutes. Stir in basil and simmer for a further 5 minutes.

Place a layer of aubergines in oiled ovenproof dish. Cover with slices of Mozzarella and spoon on a little tomato sauce. Sprinkle with Parmesan and a pinch of salt. Repeat layering, ending with Parmesan. Sprinkle a little oil over surface and bake for 15 minutes or until top begins to brown.

Turkish artichokes

Overall timing 1¼ hours

Freezing Suitable: reheat in 350°F (180°C) Gas 4 oven for 30 minutes

To serve 4

6	Small globe artichokes *or*	6
14 oz	Can of artichoke hearts	397 g
4 tbsp	Oil	4x15 ml
1	Large onion	1
1 lb	Minced beef	450 g
2 tbsp	Chopped parsley	2x15 ml
	Salt and pepper	
4	Firm tomatoes	4
4 fl oz	Stock or water	120 ml

If using fresh artichokes, break off stems, remove choke and discard hard outer leaves. Trim top third so that only tender part is left, and halve or quarter each one. Heat half the oil in frying pan, add artichokes and brown lightly. If using canned artichokes, drain them.

Peel and chop onion. Heat remaining oil in saucepan and fry onion till browned. Add minced beef and brown. Add parsley and seasoning, then cook for about 10 minutes over fairly high heat, stirring frequently to prevent burning. Add tomatoes, cut into segments, and cook for a further 5 minutes.

Grease flameproof dish and cover bottom with half the artichokes. Arrange meat mixture on top, then cover with the rest of the artichokes. Add stock or water, cover and cook gently for 30 minutes.

Neapolitan beans

Overall timing 1½ hours plus soaking

Freezing Not suitable

To serve 4

4 oz	Dried haricot beans	125 g
1	Stalk of celery	1
1	Carrot	1
1	Garlic clove	1
2 tbsp	Oil	2x15 ml
2 tbsp	Chopped parsley	2x15 ml
14 oz	Can of tomatoes	397 g
1 tbsp	Chopped fresh savory	15 ml
	Salt and pepper	
1 pint	Strong chicken stock	560 ml
8 oz	Short macaroni	225 g

Put beans in a large pan and cover with plenty of cold water. Bring to the boil and boil for 2 minutes. Remove from heat, cover and leave to soak for 2 hours.

Drain beans well, then cover with boiling water and cook for 1 hour.

Chop celery. Peel and chop carrot. Peel and crush garlic. Heat oil in a saucepan, add celery, carrot, garlic and parsley and fry for 5 minutes.

Sieve tomatoes and juice and add to vegetables with savory and seasoning. Drain beans and purée two-thirds of them in a vegetable mill or press through a sieve. Add bean purée, whole beans and stock to vegetables. Bring to the boil.

Add the macaroni and stir well. Cook for 15–20 minutes, stirring occasionally. Taste and adjust seasoning before serving.

Beef and mushroom stuffed tomatoes

Overall timing 1¼ hours

Freezing Not suitable

To serve 3–4

6	Large tomatoes	6
1	Onion	1
1 oz	Butter	25 g
1 lb	Lean minced beef	450 g
4 oz	Mushrooms	125 g
1 tbsp	Chopped parsley	15 ml
6 tbsp	Dry white wine	6x15 ml
	Salt and pepper	
1 oz	Fresh breadcrumbs	25 g
	Lemon wedges	

Preheat the oven to 350°F (180°C) Gas 4.

Halve the tomatoes and scoop out the flesh. Chop the flesh. Peel and chop the onion. Melt the butter in a frying pan and fry the onion till transparent. Add the beef and fry for 5 minutes.

Chop the mushrooms and add to the pan with the parsley, chopped tomato flesh, wine and seasoning. Cover and cook for 10 minutes.

Stir in the breadcrumbs. Spoon the mixture into the tomato halves. Arrange in an oven-proof dish and bake for 25–30 minutes till the tops are brown and crisp. Garnish with lemon wedges and serve with mashed potatoes.

Spinach omelette

Overall timing 15 minutes

Freezing Not suitable

To serve 2

6 oz	Spinach	175 g
2 oz	Butter	50 g
	Salt and pepper	
6	Eggs	6
2 tbsp	Single cream	2x15 ml

Cut away blemishes and stalks from spinach. Wash, then shred coarsely. Melt $1\frac{1}{2}$ oz (40 g) of the butter in a saucepan, add spinach and seasoning, cover and cook over a low heat for about 5 minutes till a purée.

Lightly beat the eggs in a bowl with seasoning. Melt the remaining butter in an omelette pan, add the egg mixture and cook gently till the omelette is lightly set.

Spread the spinach purée over half the omelette and spoon the cream over. Slide omelette out of the pan on to a warmed serving dish, tilting the pan so the omelette folds in half. Serve immediately with chips and a salad.

Mushroom quiche

Overall timing 50 minutes

Freezing Suitable: reheat from frozen in 350°F (180°C) Gas 4 oven for 20 minutes

To serve 6–8

13 oz	Frozen puff pastry	375 g
1 oz	Butter	25 g
12 oz	Small button mushrooms	350 g
	Salt and pepper	
3	Large eggs	3
¼ pint	Carton of single cream	150 ml
¼ pint	Milk	150 ml
¼ teasp	Grated nutmeg	1.25 ml

Thaw pastry. Preheat the oven to 425°F (220°C) Gas 7.

Roll out dough on floured surface and line 10 inch (25 cm) loose-bottomed flan tin. Prick base with fork.

Melt butter in saucepan, add mushrooms and fry for 5 minutes. Remove from heat and add plenty of seasoning. Leave to cool slightly, then spread out in flan case.

Beat eggs in a bowl with cream, milk, nutmeg and seasoning. Pour over mushrooms.

Bake for 15 minutes, then reduce heat to 350°F (180°C) Gas 4 and bake for further 15 minutes till the filling is set and the top golden. Serve hot or cold with a mixed salad.

French stuffed lettuce

Overall timing 40 minutes

Freezing Not suitable

To serve 4

4	Round lettuces	4
1 pint	Chicken stock	560 ml
2 oz	Butter	50 g
1 oz	Plain flour	25 g
$\frac{1}{2}$ pint	Milk	300 ml
	Salt	
	Grated nutmeg	
4 oz	Cooked ham	125 g
3 oz	Mozzarella cheese	75 g
2	Egg yolks	2

Preheat the oven to 350°F (180°C) Gas 4.

Trim lettuces, discarding outer leaves if necessary. Bring stock to the boil in a large saucepan. Add lettuces, cover and cook for 5 minutes. Drain thoroughly, reserving cooking liquor. Allow lettuces to cool.

Melt 1 oz (25 g) of the butter in another saucepan. Add flour and cook, stirring, for 2 minutes. Gradually stir in milk. Bring to the boil, stirring, and cook for 3 minutes. Season with salt and a pinch of grated nutmeg.

Dice ham and Mozzarella and stir into sauce with egg yolks. Cook over a low heat for 2 minutes. Remove from heat and taste and adjust seasoning.

Cut cooled lettuces in half lengthways. Arrange four lettuce halves in a greased ovenproof dish, cut sides uppermost. Spoon sauce into each half and top with remaining lettuce halves. Add $\frac{1}{4}$ pint (150 ml) of the reserved cooking liquor and dot with remaining butter.

Cover with foil and bake for 15 minutes. Serve hot with French bread.

Tunisian stuffed courgettes

Overall timing 1¼ hours

Freezing Suitable: bake from frozen, covered, in 350°F (180°C) Gas 4 oven for about 45 minutes

To serve 4

1 lb	Courgettes	450 g
1	Onion	1
8 oz	Minced lamb	225 g
1 tbsp	Chopped parsley	15 ml
2	Eggs	2
	Cayenne	
	Salt and pepper	
4 tbsp	Plain flour	4x15 ml
4 tbsp	Oil	4x15 ml
8 oz	Can of tomatoes	227 g
	Parsley	

Trim courgettes. Using a long thin knife or melon-baller, scoop out centre of each whole courgette, working from both ends if necessary and trying to keep the sides an even thickness. Reserve cut-out flesh.

Peel and finely chop onion and mix with chopped courgette flesh, minced lamb, parsley, 1 egg, a pinch of cayenne and seasoning.

Fill courgettes with prepared mixture. Roll any leftover mixture into little meat balls. Beat remaining egg in a bowl and dip stuffed courgettes and meat balls in it. Coat lightly with flour.

Heat oil in a large frying pan. Add courgettes and meat balls and cook for about 20 minutes, turning to brown all sides. Remove from pan and drain on kitchen paper.

Sieve tomatoes and their juice. Add to pan juices with seasoning and cook over a moderate heat for about 15 minutes.

Return courgettes and meat balls to pan and cook for a further 15 minutes. Serve hot, sprinkled with chopped parsley.

Fish-stuffed potatoes

Overall timing 1¾ hours

Freezing Not suitable

To serve 8

8	Large potatoes	8
2 oz	Butter	50 g
¼ pint	Carton of single cream	150 ml
2x7 oz	Cans of tuna fish	2x200 g
4 oz	Shelled prawns	125 g
2 tbsp	Chopped fresh tarragon	2x15 ml
	Salt and pepper	

Preheat the oven to 375°F (190°C) Gas 5.

Scrub the potatoes and dry. Bake for 1–1¼ hours or until tender.

Wrap each potato in a twist of foil so only the top shows. Make a deep cut along the top of each and scoop out some of the flesh into a bowl. Beat in the butter and cream. Drain and flake the tuna, then add to the mixture with the prawns, half the tarragon and seasoning. Pile into the potatoes.

Bake for a further 20 minutes. Garnish with the remaining tarragon.

Potato and bacon pan fry

Overall timing 1 hour

Freezing Not suitable

To serve 4

2 lb	Medium waxy potatoes	900 g
	Salt and pepper	
8 oz	Smoked streaky bacon rashers	225 g
1	Large onion	1
2 oz	Butter	50 g

Cook the potatoes in boiling salted water for about 30 minutes till tender.

Meanwhile, derind and dice the bacon. Peel and thinly slice the onion. Melt the butter in a frying pan and fry the onion and bacon lightly.

Drain the potatoes. Peel and slice thinly, then halve slices. Add to the frying pan, season and fry for 5 minutes, turning carefully.

Press the potatoes down into the pan, cover and fry over a moderate heat for a further 10 minutes till the outside is golden.

Run a spatula around the edge of the pan to loosen the mixture. Invert on to a warmed serving plate and serve immediately with fried eggs.

Stuffed celeriac

Overall timing 1½ hours

Freezing Not suitable

To serve 4

4	Bulbs of celeriac	4
	Salt and pepper	
1 tbsp	Lemon juice	15 ml
2 oz	Streaky bacon	50 g
1	Large onion	1
8 oz	Minced beef	225 g
1 oz	Fresh breadcrumbs	25 g
1 oz	Grated Parmesan cheese	25 g

Cook celeriac in boiling salted water with lemon juice for 20 minutes. Drain and allow to cool slightly, then cut off tops and reserve. Scoop out insides and reserve.

Preheat the oven to 400°F (200°C) Gas 6.

Derind and dice bacon, then cook for 3 minutes in frying pan. Peel and finely chop onion, cutting a few large pieces for the garnish. Fry onions till golden. Remove large pieces and set aside.

Add mince to pan and cook for 5 minutes. Chop inside of two celeriac bulbs and add to pan with breadcrumbs, Parmesan and seasoning.

Fill celeriac with meat mixture. Replace tops, then place in greased ovenproof dish. Bake for 40 minutes, basting with pan juices halfway through. Serve garnished with reserved onion pieces.

Spanish stuffed peppers

Overall timing 1 hour

Freezing Suitable: bake for 1 hour

To serve 4

1 lb	Tomatoes	450 g
1	Onion	1
1	Garlic clove	1
¼ pint	Olive oil	150 ml
1 tbsp	Caster sugar	15 ml
	Pinch of cayenne	
½ teasp	Dried oregano	2.5 ml
	Salt and pepper	
8	Firm green peppers	8
14 oz	Smoked bacon	400 g
4 oz	Fresh breadcrumbs	125 g

Blanch, peel and chop tomatoes. Peel and chop onion. Peel and crush garlic. Heat 2 tbsp (2x15 ml) oil in saucepan, add tomatoes, onion, garlic, sugar, cayenne, oregano and seasoning. Simmer till reduced by half.

Cut off stalk end of each pepper, then deseed. Blanch in boiling salted water for 5 minutes, then drain.

Preheat the oven to 400°F (200°C) Gas 6.

To make stuffing, derind and mince bacon. Mix with crumbs and pepper to taste.

Pour 1 teasp (5 ml) oil into each pepper, then fill with stuffing. Pour remaining oil into ovenproof dish. Place peppers in dish with tomato sauce between them. Cover with foil and bake for 45 minutes.

Aubergine boxes

Overall timing 1½ hours

Freezing Not suitable

To serve 4

1 lb	Aubergines	450 g
	Salt and pepper	
3	Anchovy fillets	3
2 oz	Mozzarella cheese	50 g
1 teasp	Dried basil	2x5 ml
2 teasp	Capers	2x5 ml
1	Large onion	1
2	Garlic cloves	2
2 tbsp	Oil	2x15 ml
14 oz	Can of tomatoes	397 g
1 tbsp	Worcestershire sauce	15 ml
4–5	Fresh tomatoes (optional)	4–5

Cook aubergines in boiling salted water for 5 minutes. Drain and leave to cool, then cut off stalks and make a lengthways cut through the aubergines leaving the halves still attached at one side. Ease open and remove most of the flesh with a teaspoon. Finely chop or mash the flesh and put into a bowl.

Drain and chop anchovies. Dice Mozzarella. Mix together aubergine flesh, anchovies, basil, Mozzarella, capers and seasoning. Stuff the hollowed-out aubergine shells with mixture.

Preheat the oven to 350°F (180°C) Gas 4. Peel and chop onion. Peel and crush garlic. Heat oil in flameproof casserole and fry onion till brown. Stir in garlic, tomatoes, Worcestershire sauce and seasoning. Simmer gently for about 10 minutes or until the sauce has become quite "mushy".

Arrange the stuffed aubergines on top of sauce and bake for 45 minutes. You can add 4–5 fresh tomatoes about 15 minutes before the end of the cooking time – they add attractive colour as well as taste.

Swiss chard pie

Overall timing 1¼ hours

Freezing Not suitable

To serve 6

12 oz	Frozen puff pastry	350 g
2 lb	Swiss chard stalks	900 g
	Salt and pepper	
5	Eggs	5
¾ pint	Milk	400 ml
¼ pint	Carton of single cream	150 ml
8 oz	Cheese	225 g
¼ teasp	Grated nutmeg	1.25 ml

Thaw pastry. Preheat the oven to 425°F (220°C) Gas 7.

Cut the swiss chard stalks into 2 inch (5 cm) lengths. Cook, covered, in boiling salted water for 10 minutes till tender.

Roll out two-thirds of the dough on a floured surface and use to line a 9 inch (23 cm) pie dish. Drain the chard thoroughly and arrange in the pastry case.

Beat 4 of the eggs in a bowl. Add the milk, cream, grated cheese, seasoning and nutmeg and mix together with a fork. Pour over the chard.

Brush the edges of the pastry case with water. Roll out the remaining dough and use to cover the pie. Seal, trim and crimp the edges. Decorate the top with dough trimmings. Beat the remaining egg and brush over the pie.

Place the pie on a heated baking tray and bake for 20 minutes. Reduce the temperature to 350°F (180°C) Gas 4 and bake for a further 20 minutes till well risen and golden. Serve hot.

Cowboy's pork and beans

Overall timing 50 minutes

Freezing Not suitable

To serve 4

1½ lb	Belly of pork rashers	700 g
1	Large onion	1
2 tbsp	Oil	2x15 ml
2	Garlic cloves	2
¼ teasp	Chilli powder	1.25 ml
2 tbsp	Black treacle	2x15 ml
1 tbsp	Vinegar	15 ml
½ teasp	Powdered mustard	2.5 ml
2 tbsp	Tomato ketchup	2x15 ml
½ pint	Chicken stock	300 ml
	Salt and pepper	
2x14 oz	Cans of haricot beans	2x397 g

Preheat the oven to 425°F (220°C) Gas 7.

Cut the pork into ½ inch (12.5 mm) pieces, discarding any bones. Place in roasting tin with no extra fat. Cook in the oven for about 20 minutes till crisp and golden.

Meanwhile, peel and finely chop the onion. Heat the oil in a flameproof casserole and fry the onion till transparent. Peel and crush the garlic and add to the pan with the chilli powder. Fry, stirring, for 2 minutes.

Stir in the treacle, vinegar, mustard, ketchup and chicken stock. Bring to the boil, season and simmer for 5 minutes.

Drain and rinse the canned beans and add to the sauce.

Remove the pork from the oven and reduce the temperature to 350°F (180°C) Gas 4. Add the pork pieces to the beans with 1 tbsp (15 ml) of the fat from the tin. Put the casserole in the oven and cook for about 15 minutes, stirring once, till liquid is reduced by half. Taste and adjust the seasoning, then serve immediately with a tomato and onion salad and crusty bread.

Courgettes à la provençale

Overall timing 45 minutes

Freezing Not suitable

To serve 4

1½ lb	Courgettes	700 g
2	Onions	2
2	Garlic cloves	2
1 lb	Tomatoes	450 g
2 tbsp	Oil	2 x 15 ml
	Bouquet garni	
	Salt and pepper	
4 oz	Gruyère cheese	125 g
2 tbsp	Chopped parsley	2 x 15 ml
¼ pint	Red wine	150 ml
1 oz	Butter	25 g

Slice courgettes. Peel and chop onions. Peel and crush garlic. Blanch, peel and chop tomatoes.

Heat the oil in a frying pan. Add garlic and courgettes and fry on both sides until golden. Remove from pan with draining spoon and reserve.

Add onions, tomatoes, bouquet garni and seasoning to the frying pan. Cook gently for 15 minutes, stirring from time to time.

Preheat the oven to 400°F (200°C) Gas 6.

Grate the cheese. Discard bouquet garni from tomato sauce. Arrange courgettes, cheese, tomato sauce and parsley in layers in a greased ovenproof dish, finishing with a cheese layer. Pour wine over and dot with butter. Bake for 10–15 minutes until golden brown.

Endive soufflé

Overall timing 50 minutes

Freezing Not suitable

To serve 4

4 oz	Butter	125 g
2 tbsp	Finely chopped onion	2x15 ml
2 tbsp	Finely chopped bacon	2x15 ml
4 tbsp	Diced cooked potato	4x15 ml
2 tbsp	Plain flour	2x15 ml
½ pint	Milk	300 ml
6	Eggs	6
	Salt and pepper	
6 tbsp	Chopped endive	6x15 ml

Preheat the oven to 375°F (190°C) Gas 5.

Melt 2 oz (50 g) of the butter in a frying pan. Add onion and bacon and fry till onion is transparent. Drain mixture in a sieve. Add the diced potato and set aside.

Melt the remaining butter in the frying pan, stir in the flour and cook for 1 minute. Gradually stir in the milk and bring to the boil, stirring. Simmer for 3 minutes, then remove from heat and cool slightly.

Separate the eggs. Beat yolks into the sauce, then fold in the potato and bacon mixture and seasoning. Whisk the egg whites in a bowl till stiff. Stir 1 tbsp (15 ml) of the whites into the sauce to lighten it. Stir in the endive, then carefully fold in the remaining egg whites.

Turn the mixture into a greased 6 inch (15 cm) soufflé dish and bake for 25–30 minutes till the soufflé is well risen and golden in colour. Serve immediately.

Italian fried vegetables

Overall timing 1 hour

Freezing Not suitable

To serve 6

1	Large aubergine	1
	Salt and pepper	
8 oz	Courgettes	225 g
$\frac{1}{2}$	Cauliflower	$\frac{1}{2}$
8 oz	Large flat mushrooms	225 g
2	Large dessert apples	2
4	Eggs	4
6 oz	Fine breadcrumbs	175 g
3 oz	Plain flour	75 g
	Oil for deep frying	
	Sprigs of parsley	

Cut aubergine into $\frac{1}{4}$ inch (6 mm) thick slices. Sprinkle with salt and leave for 15 minutes.

Meanwhile, halve courgettes lengthways, then cut into 2 inch (5 cm) lengths. Divide cauliflower into florets. Blanch in boiling salted water for 3 minutes, then drain and rinse under cold water.

Quarter mushrooms. Peel and core apples and cut into thick rings. Rinse aubergines and pat dry with kitchen paper.

Beat eggs in shallow dish and spread breadcrumbs on a board. Coat vegetables in seasoned flour, then dip into egg and bread-crumbs.

Heat oil in a deep-fryer to 340°F (170°C). Fry aubergine slices for about 4 minutes, turning occasionally, till crisp and golden. Drain on kitchen paper and keep hot.

Fry courgettes and cauliflower florets for 5–6 minutes, and mushrooms and apples for 3–4 minutes. Drain on kitchen paper and keep hot.

Arrange all the fried vegetables on a warmed serving dish and garnish with parsley. Serve immediately with Tartare sauce and a green salad.

Dutch baked cabbage

Overall timing 45 minutes

Freezing Not suitable

To serve 4

1	White cabbage	1
8 fl oz	Hot stock	220 ml
8 fl oz	Water	220 ml
1	Bay leaf	1
1	Garlic clove	1
1	Onion	1
2	Cloves	2
	Salt and pepper	
2 oz	Butter	50 g
3 tbsp	Plain flour	3x15 ml
1 teasp	Curry powder	5 ml
8 fl oz	Carton of single cream	227 ml
2 tbsp	Ground hazelnuts or breadcrumbs	2x15 ml

Preheat the oven to 425°F (220°C) Gas 7.

Cut out core and remove tough outer leaves of cabbage. Stand cabbage upright in a saucepan. Pour over stock and water and add bay leaf, garlic and onion spiked with cloves. Season with salt and pepper.

Bring to the boil, then cover and simmer for about 10 minutes. Carefully lift out the cabbage and cut it into wedges. Place these in a greased ovenproof dish. Reserve ½ pint (300 ml) of the strained cooking liquor.

Melt the butter in a saucepan. Stir in the flour and curry powder and cook for 1 minute. Gradually stir in the reserved cooking liquor and bring to the boil. Simmer, stirring, till thickened. Season sauce with salt, add cream and cook gently for a further 5 minutes, stirring all the time.

Pour sauce over cabbage and sprinkle top with hazelnuts or breadcrumbs. Bake for 15 minutes till top is lightly browned.

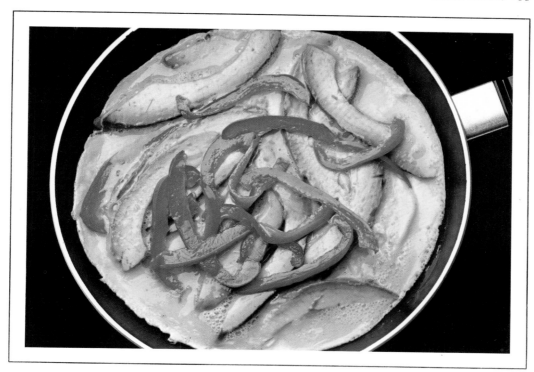

Avocado and pepper omelette

Overall timing 15 minutes

Freezing Not suitable

To serve 4

1	Red pepper	1
3 oz	Butter	75 g
2	Ripe avocados	2
1 tbsp	Lemon juice	15 ml
8	Eggs	8
1 tbsp	Water	15 ml
	Salt and pepper	

Deseed pepper and cut into long strips. Melt 1 oz (25 g) of the butter in an omelette or frying pan and fry pepper till just tender. Remove from pan and set aside.

Cut avocados in half lengthways and lift out stones. Peel, then cut avocado flesh into thick strips. Sprinkle with lemon juice to prevent discoloration.

Lightly beat together eggs, water and seasoning in a jug. Divide remaining butter into four pieces. Melt one piece in omelette pan.

Pour one-quarter of egg mixture into pan and cook till omelette starts to set. Run a spatula round the edge to loosen it and tilt the pan to let the uncooked egg run underneath. Continue to cook till the omelette is just soft and creamy.

Spread one-quarter of the pepper and avocado strips on top. Cook for 1 further minute, then fold over the omelette and slide it on to a warm serving plate. Serve immediately or keep it warm while you cook three more omelettes in the same way.

Swiss style potatoes

Overall timing 1 hour

Freezing Not suitable

To serve 4

2 lb	Potatoes	900 g
3 tbsp	Caraway seeds	3x15 ml
1 tbsp	Sea-salt	15 ml
2 oz	Butter	50 g
8 oz	Curd cheese	225 g
4 fl oz	Milk	120 ml
1	Onion	1
2 tbsp	Chopped parsley	2x15 ml
2 tbsp	Chopped mustard and cress	2x15 ml
	Salt and pepper	
Garnish		
	Parsley sprigs	
	Mustard and cress	

Preheat the oven to 350°F (180°C) Gas 4.

Halve potatoes. Mix caraway seeds and sea-salt together in a bowl. Dip the cut sides of potatoes into mixture. Place potatoes in greased ovenproof dish with the caraway seeds facing up.

Melt the butter and pour a little over each potato half. Bake for 45 minutes.

Mix cheese with milk in a bowl. Peel and finely chop onion and add to bowl with parsley, mustard and cress and seasoning.

Divide cheese mixture between warmed serving plates and place the potatoes on top. Garnish with parsley and cress.

Lentils with courgettes and potatoes

Overall timing 1½ hours

Freezing Not suitable

To serve 6

8 oz	Continental lentils	225 g
	Salt and pepper	
2	Bay leaves	2
1	Onion	1
2 tbsp	Oil	2x15 ml
12 oz	Courgettes	350 g
1	Garlic clove	1
2 tbsp	Lemon juice	2x15 ml
5	Fennel leaves	5
	Basil leaves	
	Sprig of rosemary	
1 teasp	Cumin seed	5 ml
8 oz	Potatoes	225 g
1 oz	Butter	25 g
	Chopped parsley	

Put lentils in a large saucepan. Add 2 pints (1.1 litres) water, seasoning and bay leaves. Bring to the boil and simmer for 5 minutes, then drain, reserving the liquid.

Peel and finely chop onion. Heat oil in a large saucepan and fry onion till transparent. Trim and thickly slice courgettes. Add to pan and stir-fry for 5 minutes. Peel and crush garlic and add to pan with lentils and lemon juice.

Finely chop fennel leaves and add to pan with a few basil leaves, a sprig of rosemary, the cumin and reserved lentil liquor. Simmer for 45 minutes.

Meanwhile, peel potatoes and cut into large chunks. Add to pan and simmer for a further 20 minutes or till the lentils are cooked.

Add the butter, and taste and adjust seasoning. Sprinkle with chopped parsley and serve hot with grated cheese or slices of boiled bacon.

Scalloped artichokes

Overall timing 1¾ hours

Freezing Not suitable

To serve 6

2 lb	Jerusalem artichokes	900 g
1 lb	Leeks	450 g
	Salt and pepper	
2 oz	Butter	50 g
½ pint	Carton of single cream	284 ml
½ teasp	Grated nutmeg	2.5 ml
3 tbsp	Grated Parmesan cheese	3 x 15 ml
1 tbsp	Chopped parsley	15 ml

Preheat the oven to 350°F (180°C) Gas 4.

Peel and thinly slice the artichokes. Trim and slice the leeks. Arrange vegetables in alternating thin layers in a greased oven-proof dish, seasoning each layer. Finish with a layer of artichokes.

Dot with butter. Pour cream over and sprinkle with nutmeg. Cover dish and bake for 1½ hours.

Remove lid, sprinkle with Parmesan and parsley and serve immediately.

Venetian green beans

Overall timing 1¼ hours

Freezing Suitable

To serve 4–6

1¼ lb	Runner or French beans	600 g
1 lb	Fresh tomatoes *or*	450 g
14 oz	Can of tomatoes	397 g
1	Medium onion	1
1	Garlic clove	1
·2 oz	Butter *or*	50 g
2 tbsp	Oil	2x15 ml
	Bouquet garni	
¼ teasp	Dried oregano or marjoram	1.25 ml
	Salt and pepper	

Top and tail beans and remove strings, if necessary. If using fresh tomatoes, blanch, peel and chop them; drain and chop canned tomatoes. Peel and chop the onion. Peel and crush garlic.

Heat the butter or oil in a saucepan and fry the onion till browned. Add beans, tomatoes, garlic, bouquet garni, oregano or marjoram and seasoning. Cover and simmer over a very low heat for 1 hour. If necessary add a little boiling water during cooking to prevent sticking. Serve hot.

Lyonnaise beans

Overall timing 1 hour plus soaking

Freezing Not suitable

To serve 6

12 oz	Dried butter beans	350 g
	Salt and pepper	
2	Medium onions	2
2 oz	Butter	50 g
1 tbsp	Chopped parsley	15 ml

Soak beans in water to cover overnight. Drain.

Place beans in saucepan and add $1\frac{3}{4}$ pints (1 litre) fresh water. Cover and cook for about 1 hour till tender. Add a little salt towards the end of cooking time.

Peel and finely chop onions. Melt the butter in a saucepan and add the onions, parsley and seasoning. Cook gently till onions are transparent.

Drain beans well, then toss them in the onion and parsley mixture. Transfer to a warmed serving dish and serve.

Sicilian broad beans

Overall timing 1 hour 20 minutes plus optional cooking

Freezing Not suitable

To serve 4

12 oz	Fresh broad beans	350 g
12 oz	Fresh peas	350 g
1	Small onion	1
2 tbsp	Oil	2x15 ml
4 tbsp	Water or stock	4x15 ml
	Pinch of grated nutmeg	
	Salt and pepper	
4	Canned artichoke hearts	4
6	Leaves of fresh mint	6
½ teasp	Sugar	2.5 ml
2 teasp	Vinegar	2x5 ml

Shell beans and peas. Peel and chop onion. Heat oil in a saucepan and fry onion till transparent. Add beans, peas, water or stock, nutmeg and seasoning. Cover the pan and simmer gently for 30 minutes.

Drain artichokes and cut into eighths. Add to pan and continue cooking for 10 minutes. Stir in mint (some whole leaves, some chopped) and cook for 5 minutes more. Leave to cool slightly before serving.

If you wish to serve this dish cold, add sugar and vinegar with the mint. Stir well, then transfer to a serving dish and leave till cold. Chill for 15 minutes before serving.

Brussels sprouts with chestnuts

Overall timing 1 hour

Freezing Not suitable

To serve 4–6

12 oz	Chestnuts	350 g
¾ pint	Hot beef stock	400 ml
1½ lb	Brussels sprouts	700 g
	Salt	
	Grated nutmeg	
2 oz	Butter	50 g

Make a cut in each chestnut with a sharp knife, then place them in a saucepan. Cover with cold water, bring to the boil and cook for 10 minutes.

Drain chestnuts and peel off both outer and inner skins. Add to the stock and simmer gently for about 20 minutes till tender.

Meanwhile, trim the sprouts and cut a cross in the base of each one. Cook in boiling salted water for 10–12 minutes till tender. Drain and season with nutmeg.

Melt the butter in a pan, then add the drained chestnuts and sprouts. Gently shake the pan to coat the vegetables with butter. Turn into a warmed serving dish and serve.

Cauliflower polonaise

Overall timing 35 minutes

Freezing Not suitable

To serve 4

1	Small cauliflower	1
	Salt	
4	Hard-boiled eggs	4
4 oz	Butter	125 g
2 tbsp	Dried breadcrumbs	2x15 ml
1 teasp	Paprika	5 ml

Trim cauliflower and cook whole in boiling salted water for about 20 minutes till just tender.

Meanwhile, shell and finely chop eggs.

Drain cauliflower. Place in a warmed serving dish and sprinkle with the eggs. Keep warm.

Melt butter in frying pan. Add breadcrumbs and paprika and stir-fry until crisp. Sprinkle over cauliflower and serve.

Sweet-sour red cabbage

Overall timing 1 hour 20 minutes

Freezing Suitable

To serve 4

2 lb	Red cabbage	about 1 kg
2 oz	Streaky bacon	50 g
1	Onion	1
1	Cooking apple	1
6	Whole allspice	6
½ teasp	Salt	2.5 ml
2 teasp	Honey	2x5 ml
3 fl oz	Red wine or wine vinegar	90 ml

Discard any damaged outer leaves from the cabbage. Quarter, cut away core and thick ribs and shred leaves.

Derind and chop bacon. Peel and chop onion. Cook bacon in flameproof casserole over a low heat until fat starts to run. Add onion and cook for 5 minutes, stirring.

Peel, core and chop apple and add to casserole with cabbage. Crush allspice and add to casserole with salt, honey and wine or vinegar. Mix well, then cover and simmer for 1 hour.

If there's too much liquid at the end of cooking time, remove the lid and continue simmering. Serve hot.

Celeriac with onions

Overall timing 50 minutes

Freezing Not suitable

To serve 4–6

1½ lb	Celeriac	700 g
	Salt and pepper	
1 tbsp	Lemon juice	15 ml
2	Medium onions	2
2 oz	Butter	50 g
1 oz	Pork dripping *or*	25 g
2 tbsp	Oil	2x15 ml
2 tbsp	Plain flour	2x15 ml
¾ pint	Chicken stock	400 ml

Peel celeriac and cut into ⅛ inch (3 mm) slices. Blanch in boiling salted water with the lemon juice for 5 minutes, then drain.

Peel and finely chop onions. Heat half the butter and all the dripping or oil in a large frying pan. Add onions and celeriac and cook till onions are transparent, turning the celeriac over once with tongs – take care not to break up the fragile slices.

Tilt the pan, sprinkle the flour over the fat and stir. Add the stock and seasoning. Move the pan to distribute the liquids evenly, then cover and cook over a very low heat for 30 minutes.

Transfer celeriac to a warmed serving dish. Strain the cooking juices, stir in remaining butter and seasoning to taste and pour over the celeriac.

Celery in yogurt sauce

Overall timing 45 minutes

Freezing Not suitable

To serve 4–6

2 lb	Green celery	900 g
	Salt and pepper	
1	Onion	1
1 oz	Bacon fat or pork dripping	25 g
2 oz	Butter	50 g
1 pint	Chicken stock	560 ml
Sauce		
$\frac{1}{2}$ oz	Butter	15 g
$\frac{1}{2}$ oz	Plain flour	15 g
$\frac{1}{4}$ pint	Soured cream	150 ml
$\frac{1}{4}$ pint	Plain yogurt	150 ml
	Grated nutmeg	
	Salt and pepper	

Trim celery and cut into short lengths. Blanch in boiling salted water for 5 minutes, then drain well.

Peel and chop onion. Heat bacon fat or dripping and butter in large frying pan and fry onion till transparent. Add the celery and sprinkle with pepper. Add the stock, cover and cook over a low heat for 20–30 minutes.

Remove from heat and drain liquid into a measuring jug. There should be $\frac{1}{2}$ pint (300 ml) – make up to this amount with a little extra stock if necessary. Keep celery warm in a serving dish.

To make sauce, melt butter in a saucepan. Stir in flour and cook for 1 minute. Gradually stir in reserved stock. Bring to the boil stirring. Add soured cream, yogurt, a pinch of nutmeg and seasoning. Stir till smooth and creamy. Pour sauce over celery and serve hot.

Deep-fried chicory

Overall timing 40 minutes

Freezing Not suitable

To serve 4

4	Heads of chicory	4
	Salt and pepper	
2 tbsp	Lemon juice	2x15 ml
	Oil for deep frying	
1	Egg	1
1 tbsp	Milk (optional)	15 ml
2 oz	Dried breadcrumbs	50 g

Blanch chicory in boiling salted water, with the lemon juice, for 10 minutes. Drain and leave on a wire rack until cool enough to handle, then pat dry with kitchen paper.

Heat oil in deep-fryer to 350°F (180°C).

Lightly beat egg in a large bowl with a pinch each of salt and pepper. If chicory heads are very large, add milk to the egg mixture to ensure there is sufficient coating mixture. Dip the chicory heads in the egg, then coat completely in the breadcrumbs.

Deep-fry coated chicory, two at a time, in the hot oil for 2–3 minutes or until golden brown. Drain on kitchen paper and keep warm while frying remaining chicory heads. Serve with any hot or cold meat and accompanied by sea-salt and butter to be added as you would with jacket potatoes – make a cross cut, add a knob of butter and freshly-ground sea-salt.

Cucumbers in cream

Overall timing 40 minutes

Freezing Not suitable

To serve 4

4	Cucumbers	4
	Salt and pepper	
2 oz	Butter	50 g
4 fl oz	Carton of single cream	113 ml

Peel the cucumbers and scoop out flesh with a melon baller. Alternatively, cut cucumbers into 1 inch (2.5 cm) cubes. Blanch cucumber pieces in boiling salted water for 5 minutes. Drain.

Melt the butter in a frying pan, add the cucumber and season. Cover and cook gently for about 20 minutes.

Stir cream into pan, heat through gently for 2 minutes and serve.

Chinese leaves and bacon

Overall timing 35 minutes

Freezing Not suitable

To serve 4

2 lb	Chinese leaves	900 g
	Salt and pepper	
8 oz	Onion	225 g
4 oz	Streaky bacon rashers	125 g
4 tbsp	Oil	4x15 ml
1	Chicken stock cube	1
4 fl oz	Boiling water	120 ml
3 teasp	Soy sauce	3x5 ml

Remove any marked outer leaves. Cut remaining leaves into quarters, then cut each piece in half again. Sprinkle with salt.

Peel and chop onion. Derind and chop bacon. Heat oil in saucepan, add onion and bacon and fry till onion is transparent. Add leaves and fry for a few minutes without browning.

Sprinkle in stock cube and boiling water. Cover and cook gently for 20 minutes.

Stir in soy sauce, then taste and adjust seasoning if necessary. Serve with roast or grilled chicken or with grilled liver.

Hungarian cauliflower

Overall timing 35 minutes

Freezing Not suitable

To serve 4

1	Cauliflower	1
	Salt and pepper	
4 oz	Bacon	125 g
4 oz	Mushrooms	125 g
2 oz	Butter	50 g
½ teasp	Paprika	2.5 ml
¼ pint	Soured cream	150 ml
2 oz	Cheddar cheese	50 g
	Chopped chives	

Preheat the oven to 425°F (220°C) Gas 7.

Separate cauliflower into florets. Cook in boiling salted water for 7–10 minutes, then drain.

Derind and dice bacon. Chop mushrooms. Melt butter in a large saucepan and fry bacon and mushrooms for a few minutes. Add paprika and seasoning, then mix in cauliflower.

Put mixture into an ovenproof dish. Pour soured cream on top and sprinkle with grated cheese. Bake for 15 minutes. Sprinkle chives and extra paprika and grated cheese on top and serve hot.

Roman style greens

Overall timing 30 minutes

Freezing Not suitable

To serve 6

1	Large garlic clove	1
3 tbsp	Olive oil	3x15 ml
4	Anchovy fillets	4
14 oz	Can of tomatoes	397 g
2 lb	Spring greens	900 g
	Salt and pepper	

Peel garlic. Heat oil in a large saucepan, add garlic and fry till pale golden. Remove from pan and discard.

Finely chop anchovies and add to pan with tomatoes and juice. Stir to break up tomatoes. Bring to the boil and simmer for 15 minutes.

Meanwhile, cut greens into shreds. Cook in boiling salted water for 5 minutes till tender. Drain thoroughly and add to the tomato sauce with plenty of pepper. Stir over a low heat for 5 minutes till the greens are coated with the sauce. Adjust the seasoning to taste and serve hot.

Deep-fried courgettes

Overall timing $2\frac{1}{4}$ hours

Freezing Not suitable

To serve 4

$1\frac{1}{4}$ lb	Courgettes	600 g
	Salt	
3 tbsp	Plain flour	3x15 ml
	Oil for frying	

Trim courgettes and cut into thin strips. Sprinkle with salt and leave for $1\frac{1}{2}$ hours.

Dry courgettes well on kitchen paper and coat in flour. Shake in a sieve to remove excess flour.

Heat oil in a deep-fryer.

Fry courgettes till lightly golden, then drain well on kitchen paper. Serve hot with tartare sauce.

Variations

Season the flour with a little paprika or ground coriander before coating courgettes.

Braised fennel

Overall timing 1 hour

Freezing Suitable

To serve 6

5	Bulbs of fennel	5
	Salt and pepper	
4 oz	Streaky bacon	125 g
1	Onion	1
2 oz	Butter	50 g
½ pint	Chicken stock	300 ml
	Bouquet garni	
	Sprigs of parsley	

Trim fennel. Cut each bulb in half and blanch in boiling salted water for 10 minutes. Drain.

Derind and finely chop bacon. Peel and chop onion. Melt butter in flameproof casserole and fry bacon for 5 minutes.

Arrange onion and fennel pieces on top of bacon. Cover with stock and add bouquet garni and seasoning. Cover and simmer for about 45 minutes till tender.

Remove bouquet garni. If liked, sprinkle fennel with grated Parmesan cheese. Garnish with parsley and serve with chicken or a bacon joint.

Endive ring

Overall timing 1 hour

Freezing Not suitable

To serve 4

2 lb	Curly endive	900 g
	Salt and pepper	
2 oz	Butter	50 g
2 oz	Plain flour	50 g
$\frac{3}{4}$ pint	Milk	400 ml
	Grated nutmeg	
3	Eggs	3

Trim the endive and blanch in boiling salted water for 5 minutes. Plunge pan into cold water to cool quickly, then drain endive well and chop.

Preheat the oven to 325°F (170°C) Gas 3.

Melt butter in a saucepan, stir in flour and cook for 1 minute. Gradually stir in the milk. Bring to the boil, stirring, and simmer till thickened. Season with salt, pepper and nutmeg.

Remove pan from heat and stir in endive. Allow to cool slightly, then beat eggs into mixture. Turn into greased ring mould. Place mould in roasting tin with 1 inch (2.5 cm) water. Bake for 30 minutes. Invert on to a warmed serving dish and serve hot.

Braised lettuce

Overall timing 40 minutes

Freezing Not suitable

To serve 4

4	Small round lettuces	4
	Salt and pepper	
2	Onions	2
2	Carrots	2
4 oz	Streaky bacon rashers	125 g
1 oz	Butter	25 g
½ pint	Chicken stock	300 ml

Trim lettuces. Blanch in boiling salted water for 2 minutes, then drain thoroughly.

Peel and slice onions and carrots. Derind and thinly slice bacon. Melt butter in saucepan, add onions, carrots and bacon and fry gently for 10 minutes, stirring occasionally.

Pour in stock and add blanched lettuces and seasoning. Cover and simmer for 20 minutes.

Transfer bacon and vegetables to warmed serving dish and keep hot. Boil cooking liquor rapidly to reduce by half. Taste and adjust seasoning. Pour over lettuce and serve immediately with roast meats.

Lemon-braised leeks

Overall timing 1 hour

Freezing Not suitable

To serve 4

2 lb	Leeks	900 g
	Salt and pepper	
2	Carrots	2
1	Onion	1
3 oz	Butter	75 g
¼ pint	Stock	150 ml
2 tbsp	Plain flour	2x15 ml
½	Lemon	½

Preheat the oven to 350°F (180°C) Gas 4.

Trim leeks and blanch in boiling salted water for 5 minutes. Drain.

Peel and chop carrots. Peel and slice onion. Melt 1 oz (25 g) of the butter in a flameproof casserole and fry the carrots and onion till golden. Arrange leeks on top and add stock and seasoning.

Cream remaining butter with the flour to make a paste. Squeeze juice from lemon and work into the mixture with a fork. Spread over the leeks. Cover and cook in oven for 30–35 minutes. Serve with side dish of grated cheese and chunks of brown bread.

Marseilles marrow

Overall timing 45 minutes

Freezing Not suitable

To serve 6

1½ lb	Marrow	700 g
	Salt and pepper	
12 oz	Ripe tomatoes	350 g
2	Large onions	2
3 tbsp	Olive oil	3x15 ml
4 oz	Long grain rice	125 g
1 pint	Water	560 ml
1 tbsp	Chopped parsley	15 ml

Blanch marrow in boiling salted water for 10 minutes. Drain thoroughly. Cut in half lengthways, then cut across each half into 1 inch (2.5 cm) thick slices, removing the seeds.

Blanch, peel and halve the tomatoes. Peel and slice the onions. Heat the oil in a flameproof casserole and fry onions till pale golden.

Add the rice to the casserole and fry, stirring, for 2 minutes till the oil is absorbed. Add the water, tomatoes, marrow and seasoning. Bring to the boil, then cover and simmer gently for 15–20 minutes till rice is tender and most of the water has been absorbed.

Taste and adjust the seasoning, sprinkle with parsley and serve hot.

Moravian mushrooms

Overall timing 30 minutes

Freezing Not suitable

To serve 6

1¼ lb	Button mushrooms	600 g
1 oz	Butter	25 g
½ teasp	Salt	2.5 ml
1 teasp	Cumin seeds	5 ml
1 tbsp	Finely chopped parsley	15 ml
1 tbsp	Plain flour	15 ml
1 teasp	Vinegar or lemon juice	5 ml
4 fl oz	Milk	120 ml
2 tbsp	Double cream	2x15 ml

Trim and slice the mushrooms.

Melt the butter in a saucepan and add the mushrooms, salt, cumin seeds and chopped parsley. Stir-fry over a high heat for 5 minutes, then stir in flour.

Gradually add vinegar or lemon juice and milk, stirring constantly. Lower the heat and simmer for 10 minutes, stirring frequently. Stir in cream and serve.

Onions with white wine

Overall timing 45 minutes

Freezing Not suitable

To serve 6

2 lb	Medium onions	900 g
2 oz	Butter	50 g
½ teasp	Caster sugar	2.5 ml
	Salt and pepper	
1 tbsp	Plain flour	15 ml
½ pint	Dry white wine	300 ml
2	Garlic cloves	2
	Sprig of thyme	
1 tbsp	Lemon juice	15 ml
	Chopped parsley	

Peel and thinly slice the onions into rings, then separate the rings. Melt the butter in a saucepan and fry the onions over a low heat till pale golden, stirring frequently.

Add the caster sugar, seasoning and flour and fry, stirring, for 2 minutes. Gradually add the white wine and bring to the boil, stirring constantly. Add the peeled and crushed garlic, thyme and lemon juice. Cover and simmer for about 15 minutes.

Discard the thyme. Taste and adjust the seasoning, sprinkle with chopped parsley and serve hot with roast chicken or lamb.

Potato pancakes

Overall timing 45 minutes

Freezing Not suitable

To serve 4

1¼ lb	Waxy potatoes	600 g
2	Eggs	2
1 tbsp	Plain flour	15 ml
	Salt and pepper	
4 tbsp	Oil	4x15 ml

Peel the potatoes and grate coarsely into a bowl of cold water. Drain and squeeze dry in a cloth, then put into a dry bowl. Add the eggs, flour and seasoning and mix well.

Heat a little of the oil in a frying pan and add one-quarter of the potato mixture. Flatten into a pancake with the back of a fish slice and fry over a moderate heat for about 5 minutes till the edges are golden. Turn carefully and brown the other side. Remove from the pan and keep hot while rest of mixture is cooked.

Serve hot with roast or grilled meats and a green vegetable.

Russian potatoes with cream

Overall timing 1¼ hours

Freezing Not suitable

To serve 4

1½ lb	Waxy potatoes	700 g
	Salt and pepper	
2 oz	Button mushrooms	50 g
1	Small onion	1
2 oz	Butter	50 g
¼ pint	Soured cream	150 ml
2 tbsp	Chopped parsley	2x15 ml

Cook the potatoes in boiling salted water for about 30 minutes till tender. Drain and peel the potatoes, then cut into ¼ inch (6 mm) thick slices. Slice the mushrooms. Peel and thinly slice the onion.

Melt the butter in a frying pan and fry the onion till transparent. Add the mushrooms and fry for 2–3 minutes, stirring. Add the sliced potatoes and fry for 5 minutes, turning once.

Pour the cream over and season well. Turn potatoes gently till coated and continue cooking over a low heat for about 10 minutes till the potatoes have absorbed most of the cream.

Stir in the parsley, adjust the seasoning and serve hot.

Turkish potato fritters

Overall timing 50 minutes plus proving

Freezing Not suitable

To serve 4–6

8 oz	Floury potatoes	225 g
	Salt	
1 teasp	Bicarbonate of soda	5 ml
	Grated rind of ½ lemon	
10 oz	Packet of white bread mix	283 g
	Oil for deep frying	
Syrup		
14 oz	Sugar	400 g
2 tbsp	Lemon juice	2 x 15 ml
1 tbsp	Rose-water or liqueur	15 ml

Peel and quarter potatoes. Cook in boiling salted water for 20 minutes till tender. Drain and mash. Beat in soda and lemon rind.

Put bread mix into a bowl and mix in mashed potatoes. Gradually add sufficient warm water to make a thick, smooth dough. Turn on to a floured board and knead till little bubbles appear on the surface. Place in a bowl, cover with oiled polythene and leave to rise in a warm place for about 1 hour till doubled in size.

Meanwhile, to make the syrup, place sugar in a saucepan with ¾ pint (400 ml) water, lemon juice and rose-water or liqueur and heat till sugar dissolves. Bring to the boil and boil gently for 15 minutes till syrupy. Remove from heat and keep warm.

Heat oil in a deep-fryer to 360°F (180°C).

Break off lumps of dough with a spoon and lower into oil on a draining spoon. Fry for 3–5 minutes, turning once, till golden all over. Remove and drain on kitchen paper. Keep hot while you fry the rest. Put in a deep dish and pour warm syrup over.

Paprika sauerkraut

Overall timing 50 minutes

Freezing Not suitable

To serve 6

2 oz	Streaky bacon	50 g
2	Onions	2
2 oz	Lard	50 g
2 lb	Sauerkraut	900 g
14 oz	Can of tomatoes	397 g
1 tbsp	Paprika	15 ml
1 teasp	Caraway seeds	5 ml
	Salt	
2	Potatoes	2
2	Garlic cloves	2
2	Frankfurters	2
$\frac{1}{4}$ pint	Soured cream	150 ml

Derind and dice the bacon. Peel and finely chop the onions. Melt the lard in a saucepan and fry the bacon and onions for 5 minutes. Add the sauerkraut.

Press the tomatoes through a sieve into the pan. Add the paprika, caraway seeds and salt.

Peel and grate the potatoes. Peel and crush garlic. Add both to the pan and mix well. Cover and simmer for 15 minutes.

Meanwhile, cut the frankfurters into thin slices. Add to the pan and simmer for a further 10 minutes.

Taste and adjust the seasoning. Pour into a warmed serving dish and spoon the soured cream over. Serve hot with roast or grilled meats.

Spinach dumplings

Overall timing 40 minutes plus setting

Freezing Suitable: cook from frozen for 12–15 minutes, then add melted butter and cheese.

To serve 6

2 lb	Spinach	900 g
$\frac{1}{2}$	Chicken stock cube	$\frac{1}{2}$
5 tbsp	Warm milk	5 x 15 ml
12 oz	Plain flour	350 g
3	Eggs	3
	Salt and pepper	
4 oz	Butter	125 g
8 oz	Fresh breadcrumbs	225 g
$\frac{1}{4}$ teasp	Grated nutmeg	1.25 ml
1 tbsp	Chopped parsley	15 ml
1 tbsp	Chopped chives	15 ml
4 oz	Emmenthal cheese	125 g

Wash spinach and put into a saucepan with only water that clings to it. Cover and cook for 5 minutes.

Dissolve stock cube in milk. Sift flour into a bowl, add eggs, milk and seasoning and mix to a soft dough.

Drain spinach thoroughly and chop finely. Melt half the butter in a frying pan, add breadcrumbs and fry till crisp and golden. Add to dough with nutmeg, parsley and chives. Add spinach and mix to a stiff dough.

Roll dough between floured hands into long sausage-shapes about $\frac{1}{2}$ inch (12.5 mm) in diameter. Leave to set.

Cut across dough into 1 inch (2.5 cm) lengths. Cook in boiling salted water for about 10 minutes till they float to the surface.

Lift out dumplings with a draining spoon, drain thoroughly and arrange in a warmed serving dish. Melt remaining butter, pour over dumplings and sprinkle with grated cheese. Toss lightly before serving with casseroles.

Sweetcorn fritters

Overall timing 30 minutes

Freezing Not suitable

To serve 4

1 lb	Can of sweetcorn kernels	450 g
1	Egg	1
2 oz	Plain flour	50 g
	Salt	
1 tbsp	Oil	15 ml
	Grated rind of $\frac{1}{2}$ lemon	
	Oil for deep frying	
	Grated Parmesan cheese	

Drain sweetcorn. Separate egg. Sift flour and pinch of salt into a mixing bowl. Make a well in centre, then put in egg yolk, oil and grated lemon rind. Stir until a smooth batter forms.

In another bowl, whisk egg white till stiff. Fold into batter with sweetcorn.

Heat oil in deep-fryer to 340°F (170°C).

Drop spoonfuls of batter into the hot oil – be careful because corn can burst – a few at a time, and fry for 5 minutes on each side or until golden. Remove with a fish slice and drain on kitchen paper. Keep warm while frying the rest.

Sprinkle grated Parmesan over and serve hot.

Mixed vegetables in milk

Overall timing 35 minutes

Freezing Not suitable

To serve 4

1	Large potato	1
1	Bulb of celeriac	1
2	Carrots	2
1	Turnip	1
1	Small cauliflower	1
8 oz	Green beans	225 g
$\frac{3}{4}$ pint	Milk	400 ml
2 oz	Butter	50 g
	Salt and pepper	
2 tbsp	Plain flour	2x15 ml
4 tbsp	Single cream	4x15 ml

Peel and dice potato, celeriac, carrots and turnip. Divide cauliflower into small florets. Top and tail beans, remove strings and chop.

Heat milk with half the butter and salt. Add potato, celeriac, carrots and turnip and cook for 10 minutes. Add cauliflower and beans and cook for a further 5 minutes. Drain vegetables, reserving milk.

Melt remaining butter in pan, stir in flour and cook for 1 minute. Gradually stir in reserved milk and simmer till thickened. Add cooked vegetables and heat through. Remove from heat and stir in cream and seasoning to taste.

Peas bonne femme

Overall timing 45 minutes

Freezing Not suitable

To serve 4

2 lb	Fresh peas	900 g
6	Small onions	6
1	Round lettuce	1
1	Thick streaky bacon rasher	1
3 oz	Butter	75 g
1 tbsp	Chopped parsley	15 ml
$\frac{1}{2}$ teasp	Sugar	2.5 ml
$\frac{1}{4}$ pint	Water	150 ml
	Salt and pepper	
1 teasp	Plain flour	5 ml

Shell peas. Blanch onions in boiling water for 5 minutes, then peel. Shred lettuce. Derind and chop bacon.

Melt 2 oz (50 g) butter in a saucepan and fry peas, onions, lettuce, parsley and bacon for 3 minutes, stirring. Add sugar, water and seasoning. Bring to the boil, cover and simmer for 15–20 minutes till peas and onions are tender.

Mix flour with remaining butter to a paste and add in small pieces to the vegetable mixture, stirring constantly. Cook for 3 minutes. Taste and adjust the seasoning and serve hot.

Cheesy vegetables

Overall timing 10 minutes

Freezing Not suitable

To serve 6

8 oz	Cream cheese	225 g
¼ pint	Carton of single cream	150 ml
2 lb	Hot cooked mixed vegetables (including beans, cauliflower, peas, carrots and mushrooms)	900 g
2 tbsp	Grated Parmesan cheese	2x15 ml
	Salt and pepper	

Beat the cream cheese and cream together in a bowl. Place the bowl over a pan of simmering water and heat through gently, stirring occasionally. Do not boil.

Arrange the vegetables in a warmed serving dish. Keep hot.

Beat the Parmesan into the cream cheese mixture and season to taste. Pour the hot sauce over the vegetables and serve immediately with roast or grilled meat, or as vegetarian lunch.

Greek pumpkin

Overall timing 1 hour

Freezing Not suitable

To serve 4–6

2 lb	Pumpkin	900 g
2	Medium onions	2
3 tbsp	Olive oil	3x15 ml
14 oz	Can of tomatoes	397 g
¼ teasp	Ground cumin	1.25 ml
2	Sprigs of flat-leafed parsley	2
	Salt and pepper	
½ pint	Water	300 ml

Scrape the seeds and fibrous centre out of the pumpkin. Cut into chunks, leaving the skin on. Peel the onions and cut through the root into eight wedges.

Heat the oil in a saucepan, add onions and fry till transparent. Add the tomatoes and juice, cumin and pumpkin. Chop the parsley and add with seasoning and the water. Bring to the boil, then cover and simmer for 25–35 minutes till the pumpkin is tender.

Adjust the seasoning and pour into a warmed serving dish. Serve hot with roast or grilled meat.

Garlic endive salad

Overall timing 40 minutes

Freezing Not suitable

To serve 4

8–12	Slices of French bread	8–12
5	Garlic cloves	5
3 tbsp	Olive oil	3×15 ml
1 tbsp	Wine vinegar	15 ml
	Salt and pepper	
1	Large curly endive	1

Cut each slice of bread into large chunks and remove most of the inside (make this into breadcrumbs). Peel and halve the garlic cloves and rub over the bread crusts. Leave the pieces of garlic on the crusts for 30 minutes to allow the flavour to develop. If you prefer a stronger taste of garlic, crush it and spread over the bread. (If crusts are not fresh and crisp, fry them lightly in a mixture of oil and butter, drain and leave to cool.)

To make dressing, lightly beat together the oil and vinegar and season to taste with salt and pepper.

Wash and dry endive. Place in serving bowl, add dressing, toss and mix in the garlic crusts.

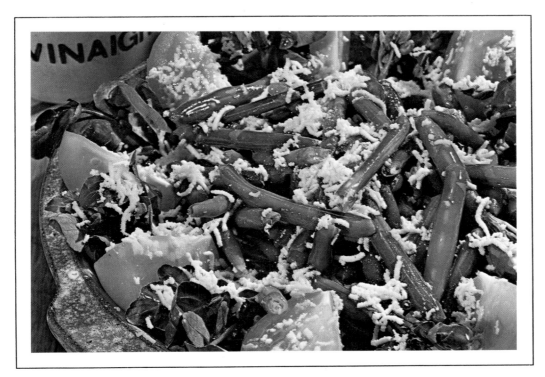

Salade Béatrice

Overall timing 10 minutes plus chilling

Freezing Not suitable

To serve 4

1 lb	Cooked green beans	450 g
	Salt and pepper	
3 tbsp	Oil	3 x 15 ml
1 tbsp	White wine vinegar	15 ml
2	Tomatoes	2
1	Bunch of watercress	1
1	Hard-boiled egg yolk	1

Break or cut the beans into short lengths and put into a salad bowl. Season, add oil and vinegar and mix together well. Chill for 15 minutes.

Cut tomatoes into quarters and arrange around the edge of the salad bowl with the watercress.

Just before serving, garnish with sieved or finely chopped egg yolk. Toss salad at the table.

Normandy salad

Overall timing 10 minutes plus chilling

Freezing Not suitable

To serve 4

1	Round lettuce	1
2	Dessert apples	2
½	Lemon	½
3 tbsp	Single cream	3x15 ml
1 tbsp	Cider vinegar	15 ml
	Grated nutmeg	
	Salt and pepper	
2 oz	Walnut halves	50 g

Wash and dry lettuce. Peel and core apples. Cut into thin rings. Rub cut surface of the lemon half over both sides of the apple rings to prevent browning. Place lettuce leaves and apple in a salad bowl and chill for 15 minutes.

Mix together the cream, cider vinegar, a pinch of grated nutmeg and seasoning in a small bowl. Just before serving, pour dressing over salad and toss. Garnish with walnut halves.

Walnut cabbage salad

Overall timing 30 minutes plus maceration

Freezing Not suitable

To serve 4

$\frac{1}{2}$	Red cabbage	$\frac{1}{2}$
4 tbsp	Walnut or olive oil	4x15 ml
2 tbsp	Lemon juice	2x15 ml
2	Large oranges	2
1	Large dessert apple	1
1	Banana	1
2 oz	Walnut halves	50 g
1 oz	Seedless raisins	25 g

Shred the cabbage and toss with the oil and lemon juice. Leave to macerate in the refrigerator for 1 hour.

Peel the oranges and separate into segments. Peel, core and chop the apple. Peel and thickly slice the banana. Add the fruit to the cabbage with the walnuts and raisins. Toss together well, then serve.

Cucumber and cider salad

Overall timing 10 minutes plus 1 hour chilling

Freezing Not suitable

To serve 4

2	Cucumbers	2
$\frac{1}{4}$ pint	Dry cider	150 ml
3 tbsp	Chopped parsley	3x15 ml
1 teasp	Sugar	5 ml
	Salt and pepper	

Peel cucumbers. Cut them in half lengthways and scoop out the seeds with a spoon. Thinly slice cucumbers and put into a bowl.

Mix together the cider, parsley, sugar and seasoning. Pour over the cucumber and chill for at least 1 hour. Toss gently before serving.

Cauliflower mayonnaise

Overall timing 30 minutes plus chilling

Freezing Not suitable

To serve 4

1	Large cauliflower	1
	Salt and pepper	
6 tbsp	Oil	6x15 ml
2 tbsp	Lemon juice	2x15 ml
3	Tomatoes	3
8	Lettuce leaves	8
$\frac{1}{4}$ pint	Thick mayonnaise	150 ml

Divide cauliflower into large florets. Cook in boiling salted water for 5–10 minutes till just tender.

Meanwhile, put the oil, lemon juice and seasoning into a bowl and mix together with a fork.

Drain the cauliflower thoroughly and add to the dressing while still hot. Toss lightly, then chill for 1 hour.

Meanwhile, slice two of the tomatoes; cut the other in half in a zigzag pattern.

Arrange six lettuce leaves on a serving dish and pile the cauliflower on top. Shred the remaining lettuce and scatter over the cauliflower. Put a tomato half on top and arrange the tomato slices round the edge.

Pipe or spoon the mayonnaise into the tomato half and between the florets. Serve immediately with cold meats or smoked fish.

Goat's cheese salad

Overall timing 15 minutes plus 1 hour chilling

Freezing Not suitable

To serve 4

12 oz	Goat's cheese	350 g
	Salt and pepper	
4 tbsp	Olive oil	4x15 ml
2 tbsp	Wine vinegar	2x15 ml
4	Stalks of celery	4
2 oz	Walnuts	50 g
	Fennel seed (optional)	

Slice cheese and put into serving bowl. Grind black pepper over it. Beat 2 tbsp (2x15 ml) oil and 1 tbsp (15 ml) vinegar together and pour over cheese.

Chop celery. Add celery and nuts to bowl. Toss lightly.

Beat together the rest of the oil and vinegar and pour over. Sprinkle with salt and crushed fennel seed, if used, and chill for 1 hour. Serve with crusty French bread.

Carrot and cabbage slaw

Overall timing 15 minutes plus chilling

Freezing Not suitable

To serve 4

8 oz	Carrots	225 g
8 oz	White cabbage	225 g
4 tbsp	Wine vinegar	4x15 ml
5 tbsp	Oil	5x15 ml
½ teasp	Caraway seeds	2.5 ml
¼ teasp	Sugar	1.25 ml
	Salt and pepper	
2 oz	Streaky bacon	50 g
1	Large onion	1

Peel and grate carrots. Shred cabbage. In a salad bowl, mix together vinegar, 4 tbsp (4x15 ml) of the oil, caraway seeds, sugar and seasoning. Add carrots and cabbage and mix well. Cover the bowl and chill for 30 minutes.

Derind and chop the bacon. Heat remaining 1 tbsp (15ml) oil in frying pan and fry bacon for 3 minutes till crisp. Peel and finely chop onion, saving a few rings for garnish. Add chopped onion to pan and fry for a few minutes.

Remove salad from refrigerator. Put the hot bacon and onion mixture on top and garnish with onion rings. Serve with roasts or cold meat.

Caesar salad

Overall timing 15 minutes plus chilling

Freezing Not suitable

To serve 4

6 tbsp	Oil	6x15 ml
2 tbsp	Vinegar	2x15 ml
2	Garlic cloves	2
	Salt and pepper	
$\frac{1}{2}$	Cos lettuce	$\frac{1}{2}$
4	Eggs	4
2	Slices of bread	2
2 oz	Roquefort or Parmesan cheese	50g
4	Anchovy fillets	4

Beat together 4 tbsp (4x15ml) of the oil, the vinegar, 1 peeled and crushed garlic clove and seasoning in a bowl. Cover and chill for 30 minutes.

Wash and dry lettuce. Tear leaves into pieces, put in a bowl and leave in the refrigerator to crisp.

Put eggs in a pan of cold water, bring to the boil and cook for 4–5 minutes. Drain and place in a bowl of cold water. Shell.

Rub bread slices all over with remaining halved garlic clove, then cut into 1 inch (2.5 cm) cubes. Fry in rest of oil till golden. Drain croûtons on kitchen paper.

Divide lettuce and croûtons between serving plates. Arrange eggs on top of lettuce, sprinkle over crumbled or grated cheese, then spoon dressing over. Garnish with rolled anchovy fillets and serve with crusty bread.

Waldorf salad

Overall timing 15 minutes plus 1 hour
refrigeration

Freezing Not suitable

To serve 4

4	Stalks of celery	4
8 oz	Dessert apples	225 g
1 tbsp	Lemon juice	15 ml
	Salt and pepper	
6 tbsp	Thick mayonnaise	6x15 ml
2 oz	Nuts	50 g

Chop celery. Peel, core and dice apples. Place
in salad bowl with celery, lemon juice and a
little salt. Chill for about 1 hour.

Remove from refrigerator and stir in mayonnaise, chopped nuts and seasoning to taste.

If serving this salad on a special occasion,
divide mixture between hollowed-out apples
that have been sprinkled with lemon juice.
For a simpler, yet still effective presentation,
serve on lettuce (shredded or leaves) in individual glass dishes and garnish with fine lemon
slices.

Chicken pineapple salad

Overall timing 30 minutes plus chilling

Freezing Not suitable

To serve 4–6

4 oz	Long grain rice	125 g
	Salt and pepper	
4 oz	Frozen sweetcorn kernels	125 g
1	Celery heart	1
1	Cold roast chicken	1
8 oz	Can of pineapple rings	227 g
4	Small firm tomatoes	4
2 oz	Black olives	50 g
3 tbsp	Salad oil	3 x 15 ml
1 tbsp	Lemon juice	15 ml
1 tbsp	Chopped chives	15 ml
1	Round lettuce	1
1	Hard-boiled egg	1

Cook the rice in boiling salted water till tender, adding the sweetcorn for the last 5 minutes of cooking. Drain and rinse under cold water, then drain thoroughly.

Trim celery heart and cut into 2 inch (5 cm) lengths. Put into a large bowl with the celery leaves. Cut the chicken into bite-size pieces, discarding the skin and bones. Add to the bowl.

Drain the pineapple; chop three of the rings. Quarter the tomatoes and add to the bowl with the chopped pineapple, olives, rice and sweetcorn.

Mix together the oil, lemon juice, chives and seasoning. Pour over the salad and toss lightly. Chill for 30 minutes.

Wash and dry the lettuce and use to line a salad bowl. Pile the salad into the centre and garnish with the remaining pineapple rings and the hard-boiled egg quartered lengthways. Serve with crusty bread.

Vegetable and herb salad

Overall timing 30 minutes

Freezing Not suitable

To serve 6

1 lb	Potatoes	450 g
	Salt and pepper	
8 oz	Cauliflower	225 g
4 oz	Green beans	125 g
4 oz	Frozen peas	125 g
4 tbsp	Oil	4x15 ml
2 tbsp	Vinegar	2x15 ml
2 tbsp	Chopped fresh mixed herbs	2x15 ml

Scrub the potatoes and cut into small chunks. Place in a saucepan, cover with water, add salt and bring to the boil. Boil gently for 2 minutes.

Divide cauliflower into florets. Add to the pan. Bring back to the boil. Cut beans into 1 inch (2.5 cm) lengths and add to pan with the peas. Simmer gently for 5 minutes or until the potatoes are tender.

Meanwhile, whisk together the oil, vinegar, herbs and seasoning.

Drain the vegetables well and place in salad bowl. While still hot, pour dressing over the vegetables and toss well. Allow to cool before serving.

Israeli sweet-sour salad

Overall timing 20 minutes plus chilling

Freezing Not suitable

To serve 4

2 tbsp	Sultanas	2x15 ml
1 lb	Carrots	450 g
4	Oranges	4
2	Avocados	4
2 tbsp	Lemon juice	2x15 ml
3 tbsp	Oil	3x15 ml
1 tbsp	Wine or cider vinegar	15 ml
	Salt and pepper	
	Ground ginger	

Put the sultanas into a bowl, cover with warm water and leave to soak.

Peel carrots and grate into serving dish. Add the juice of two of the oranges and mix well. Peel remaining oranges and separate into segments.

Peel avocados and remove stones. Cut flesh into chunks and sprinkle with lemon juice.

Drain sultanas and add to serving dish with oranges and avocados.

In a small bowl, beat the oil and vinegar with a pinch each of salt, pepper and ground ginger. Pour over salad and toss. Chill for 15 minutes before serving.

Tunisian mixed salad

Overall timing 25 minutes plus chilling

Freezing Not suitable

To serve 4

1½ lb	Cooked waxy potatoes	700 g
8 oz	Cooked carrots	225 g
3	Canned artichoke hearts	3
6 oz	Cooked peas	175 g
2 tbsp	Drained capers	2x15 ml
12	Stoned black olives	12
12	Stoned green olives	12
4 tbsp	Olive oil	4x15 ml
2 tbsp	Lemon juice	2x15 ml
1 tbsp	Chopped parsley	15 ml
¼ teasp	Ground coriander	1.25 ml
	Salt and pepper	

Dice the potatoes and carrots. Drain the artichokes and cut into quarters. Put all the vegetables into a serving dish with the capers and olives.

Whisk the oil and lemon juice together with the parsley, coriander and plenty of seasoning. Pour the dressing over the salad and toss lightly. Chill for 30 minutes before serving with crusty bread.

Beetroot and apple salad

Overall timing 1 hour 40 minutes plus cooking

Freezing Not suitable

To serve 4–6

1¾ lb	Beetroot	750 g
	Salt	
4 tbsp	Oil	4 x 15 ml
2 tbsp	Wine vinegar or lemon juice	2 x 15 ml
1 teasp	Sugar	5 ml
8 oz	Dessert apples	225 g
1	Onion	1

Wash beetroot, then cut off tops. Take care not to pierce the skin when you are preparing beetroot or the colour will boil out, leaving them a rather washed out pink. Place prepared beetroot in saucepan and cover with water. Add a little salt, cover and simmer for 1¼ hours over a low heat. Leave to cool.

Drain beetroot, cut off root and pull off skin. Slice with a mandolin or fluted grater. Dry slices and put them in layers in a salad bowl.

Mix together oil, wine vinegar or lemon juice and sugar and pour over beetroot. Chill for 2 hours.

Peel, core and chop apples. Peel and finely chop onion. Mix into beetroot and serve before the beetroot has time to colour the apple and onion.

Mimosa salad

Overall timing 15 minutes

Freezing Not suitable

To serve 4

3 tbsp	Single cream	3x15 ml
1 tbsp	Lemon juice	15 ml
	Salt and pepper	
1	Lettuce	1
1	Orange	1
4 oz	Black and white grapes	125 g
1	Banana	1
1	Hard-boiled egg yolk	1

In a salad bowl, mix together the cream, lemon juice and seasoning.

Wash and dry lettuce leaves. Peel the orange and cut into thin slices. Wash grapes. Peel and slice banana. Place the lettuce, orange, grapes and banana in salad bowl on top of dressing. Toss just before serving and garnish with sieved egg yolk.

Swiss salad

Overall timing 35 minutes

Freezing Not suitable

To serve 4

12 oz	Boiled new potatoes	350 g
1	Dessert apple	1
2 tbsp	White wine vinegar	2x15 ml
1 teasp	Made mustard	5 ml
4 tbsp	Oil	4x15 ml
	Salt and pepper	
$\frac{1}{2}$	Round lettuce	$\frac{1}{2}$
6 oz	Gruyère cheese	175 g
4	Hard-boiled eggs	4
2 teasp	Chopped chives	2x5 ml
1 teasp	Paprika	5 ml

Peel and slice the potatoes into a bowl. Peel, core and slice the apple and toss in the vinegar. Add to the potatoes.

Mix the mustard, oil and seasoning together in a bowl and pour over the potatoes and apple. Toss lightly.

Wash and dry the lettuce leaves and use to line salad bowl. Arrange the potato mixture on the lettuce.

Cut the cheese into matchsticks. Scatter the cheese round the edge and in the centre of the salad. Shell and slice the eggs and arrange on the salad. Sprinkle with the chives and paprika and serve immediately with crusty or wholemeal bread or rolls and butter.

Fennel and tomato salad

Overall timing 30 minutes

Freezing Not suitable

To serve 4

1	Large bulb of fennel	1
	Salt and pepper	
1	Onion	1
4	Tomatoes	4
3 tbsp	Oil	3x15 ml
1 tbsp	Wine vinegar or lemon juice	15 ml

Trim fennel. Cut into thin slices and blanch in boiling salted water for 5 minutes. Drain.
Peel onion and cut into rings. Slice tomatoes. Arrange fennel, onion and tomatoes in layers in salad bowl.
In another bowl, mix together oil, vinegar or lemon juice and seasoning. Pour over salad. Chill for 15 minutes before serving.

Prawn and egg salad

Overall timing 35 minutes

Freezing Not suitable

To serve 4–6

1	Lemon	1
12 oz	Shelled prawns	350 g
¼ teasp	Tabasco sauce	1.25 ml
	Salt and pepper	
4–6	Hard-boiled eggs	4–6
¼ pint	Thick mayonnaise	150 ml
1 teasp	Tomato purée	5 ml
½ teasp	Anchovy essence	2.5 ml
	Lettuce leaves	
2 oz	Black olives	50 g
4 oz	Unshelled prawns	125 g

Cut lemon in half across the segments; reserve one half. Finely grate rind of the other and reserve. Squeeze juice into a bowl.

Add shelled prawns to lemon juice with Tabasco sauce and seasoning. Leave to marinate for 15 minutes.

Meanwhile, shell eggs and cut in half lengthways. Divide the mayonnaise between two bowls. Add tomato purée and anchovy essence to one and grated lemon rind to the other.

Put the yellow mayonnaise mixture into a piping bag fitted with a star nozzle and pipe on to half the eggs. Pipe the pink mixture on to the remaining eggs.

Line a serving dish with lettuce leaves. Arrange the marinated prawns in a circle in the centre. Place eggs around the edge, alternating the colours, and garnish with the black olives.

Cut remaining lemon half into a basket shape and place in centre of the dish. Hang the whole unshelled prawns on the lemon and serve immediately.

Sweet and sour corn salad

Overall timing 45 minutes including chilling

Freezing Not suitable

To serve 6

8 oz	Can of sweetcorn kernels	225 g
2 tbsp	Wine vinegar	2x15 ml
3 tbsp	Oil	3x15 ml
	Salt and pepper	
1 lb	Cold boiled potatoes	450 g
8 oz	Tomatoes	225 g
8 oz	Can of pineapple chunks	247 g
2	Bananas	2
5 tbsp	Lemon juice	5x15 ml
1	Small lettuce	1
Dressing		
1 tbsp	French mustard	15 ml
¼ pint	Soured cream or plain yogurt	150 ml
2 tbsp	Milk	2x15 ml
	Salt and pepper	
1 teasp	Paprika	5 ml

Drain sweetcorn and place in a bowl. Mix together vinegar, oil and seasoning and add to bowl. Mix well. Cover and chill.

Peel and dice potatoes. Slice tomatoes. Drain pineapple, reserving 2 tbsp (2x15 ml) of the juice. Peel and slice bananas. Put all these in a bowl and pour lemon juice over.

Mix together dressing ingredients with reserved pineapple juice. Add to potato mixture. Chill for 30 minutes.

Line serving dish with lettuce leaves and spoon potato mixture in a ring round the edge. Pile sweetcorn in the middle and serve.

Crispy lettuce and cheese salad

Overall timing 15 minutes plus chilling

Freezing Not suitable

To serve 4–6

1	Large bulb of fennel	1
	Salt and pepper	
1	Cos lettuce	1
1	Onion	1
4 tbsp	Oil	4x15 ml
1 tbsp	Lemon juice	15 ml
3 oz	Grated Parmesan cheese	75 g
1 tbsp	Chopped parsley	15 ml

Trim fennel. Cut into small pieces and blanch in boiling salted water for 2 minutes. Drain.

Wash and dry lettuce. Shred finely. Peel and thinly slice onion. Put into a salad bowl with blanched fennel and lettuce and mix well together. Chill for 15 minutes to crisp.

Meanwhile, beat the oil and lemon juice together in a small bowl. Add salt and lots of freshly-ground black pepper.

Add Parmesan and chopped parsley to salad bowl and pour dressing over. Toss and serve immediately.

This salad makes a good accompaniment to many Italian-style dishes incorporating pasta and tomato sauce.

Rice salad with anchovy dressing

Overall timing 40 minutes plus chilling

Freezing Not suitable

To serve 4

8 oz	Long grain rice	225 g
	Salt and pepper	
1	Can of anchovy fillets	1
2	Large hard-boiled eggs	2
1 teasp	Powdered mustard	5 ml
5 tbsp	Olive oil	5 x 15 ml
1	Carrot	1
1	Small onion	1
1	Green chilli	1
1	Red pepper	1
1	Small bulb of fennel	1
2 oz	Stoned black olives	50 g
1 teasp	Chopped chives	5 ml

Cook rice in boiling salted water for 15 minutes till tender. Drain and rinse under cold water to cool.

Drain anchovies and reserve half for garnish. Put the rest into a mortar and pound to a paste with the pestle. Shell and finely chop eggs. Add to mortar with mustard and pound together, gradually adding oil a few drops at a time. Season.

Peel carrot and cut shallow grooves at intervals along its length. Slice thinly and place in large bowl with rice.

Peel and finely chop onion; thinly slice chilli: deseed and slice pepper. Add these to the rice. Thinly slice fennel; chop fennel tops and add to salad. Toss lightly. Chill salad and dressing for 30 minutes.

Put salad into a serving dish and arrange reserved anchovies on top with olives and chives. Serve with dressing.

Raw mushroom salad

Overall timing 20 minutes plus chilling

Freezing Not suitable

To serve 4

12 oz	Button mushrooms	350 g
1 teasp	Lemon juice	5 ml
1 teasp	Made mustard	5 ml
2 tbsp	Single cream	2x15 ml
2 tbsp	Oil	2x15 ml
1½ teasp	White wine vinegar	7.5 ml
	Salt and pepper	
	Chopped parsley	

Thinly slice the mushrooms. Put into a salad bowl and sprinkle with the lemon juice.

Mix together the mustard, cream, oil, vinegar and seasoning. Pour this dressing over the mushrooms and toss carefully. Sprinkle chopped parsley on top. Chill for 30 minutes before serving.

Cockle salad

Overall timing 1 hour 20 minutes

Freezing Not suitable

To serve 4

2 lb	Fresh cockles	900 g
	Coarse salt	
1	Small onion	1
$\frac{1}{4}$ pint	Dry white wine	150 ml
1	Lettuce	1
1 tbsp	Strong made mustard	15 ml
3 tbsp	Oil	3x15 ml
1 tbsp	Vinegar	15 ml
1 tbsp	Chopped parsley or chives	15 ml
	Salt and pepper	

Scrub cockles well under running cold water. Add as much coarse salt to a bowl of water as will dissolve and place the cockles in the water so that they open and release any sand or grit.

Remove cockles from bowl, then rinse under cold running water and drain.

Peel and chop onion. Put into saucepan with wine and boil till wine begins to evaporate. Add cockles and cook, stirring, for about 3 minutes till the shells open. Discard any that do not open. Strain the juice and reserve.

Line salad bowl with lettuce leaves. Remove cockles from shells and pile them on the lettuce. Mix together the reserved strained juice, mustard, oil, vinegar, parsley or chives and seasoning. Pour over cockles just before serving.

Florida salad

Overall timing 20 minutes plus chilling

Freezing Not suitable

To serve 4

1	Fresh red chilli	1
3 tbsp	Olive oil	3x15 ml
2 teasp	Vinegar	2x5 ml
	Salt and pepper	
4	Slices of fresh pineapple *or*	4
8 oz	Can of pineapple slices in natural juice	227 g
1	Red pepper	1
1	Yellow or green pepper	1
3	Medium bananas	3
1	Large avocado	1

Deseed and finely chop the chilli. Put into a bowl with the oil, vinegar and seasoning and mix well with a fork.

Peel and chop the fresh pineapple, or drain and chop the canned pineapple, and add to the bowl. Deseed and chop the peppers and add to the bowl. Peel and slice the bananas. Halve the avocado, discard the stone, peel and cut into chunks. Add to the bowl with the bananas.

Toss the salad lightly and put into a serving dish. Chill for 30 minutes before serving with chicken or seafood.

Chef's salad

Overall timing 20 minutes

Freezing Not suitable

To serve 4–6

1	Round lettuce	1
2	Heads of radicchio *or*	2
$\frac{1}{4}$	Red cabbage	$\frac{1}{4}$
4 oz	Cooked ham	125 g
3 oz	Gruyère or Emmenthal cheese	75 g
1	Small onion	1
2	Tomatoes	2
Dressing		
2 tbsp	Oil	2x15 ml
1 tbsp	Wine vinegar	15 ml
1 teasp	Dijon mustard or made English mustard	5 ml
	Salt and pepper	

Wash and dry lettuce. Line salad bowl with crisp whole leaves. Tear the rest into bite-size pieces and arrange on top.

Wash and dry radicchio and tear into pieces, or shred cabbage. Cut ham into $\frac{1}{2}$ inch (12.5 mm) dice. Slice cheese, then cut into small strips. Peel and slice onion and separate into individual rings. Cut tomatoes into wedges. Arrange all the prepared ingredients on top of the lettuce.

Mix together the dressing ingredients and pour over the salad. Toss thoroughly but gently. Garnish with garlic croûtons (see page 74), if liked.

Spanish salad

Overall timing 45 minutes plus 1 hour refrigeration

Freezing Not suitable

To serve 4

$\frac{1}{2}$	Cucumber	$\frac{1}{2}$
	Salt and pepper	
12 oz	Potatoes	350 g
12 oz	Can of asparagus spears	340 g
8 fl oz	Mayonnaise	220 ml
1 tbsp	French mustard	15 ml
$\frac{1}{2}$ teasp	Dried tarragon	2.5 ml
$\frac{1}{2}$	Red pepper	$\frac{1}{2}$

Peel and slice cucumber. Sprinkle with salt and chill for 1 hour.

Peel and dice potatoes, then cook in boiling salted water for 10 minutes. Drain and leave to cool.

Drain asparagus and dry spears on kitchen paper.

Mix together potatoes, mayonnaise, mustard, tarragon and seasoning and put into a shallow dish. Arrange asparagus on top like the spokes of a wheel. Drain cucumber slices and place one between each asparagus spear and one in the centre. Deseed and dice pepper and place on top of cucumber to add colour.

Esau's salad

Overall timing 1 hour plus cooling

Freezing Not suitable

To serve 6

1 lb	Continental lentils	450 g
2 oz	Smoked bacon	50 g
4 tbsp	Oil	4x15 ml
2	Frankfurters	2
1 tbsp	Vinegar	15 ml
1 teasp	Made mustard	5 ml
	Salt and pepper	
1	Onion	1
1	Green pepper	1
2	Tomatoes	2
2	Hard-boiled eggs	2
1 tbsp	Chopped parsley or chives	15 ml

Put lentils in a saucepan and add enough water just to cover. Bring to the boil, cover and simmer for about 1 hour till tender. Drain and leave to cool.

Derind bacon and cut into strips. Heat 1 tbsp (15 ml) of the oil in a frying pan, add bacon and cook until golden. Remove from pan and allow to cool.

Put frankfurters in a pan, cover with water and bring to the boil. Drain and leave to cool.

Meanwhile, beat together the rest of the oil, the vinegar, mustard and seasoning in a serving dish.

Peel and slice onion. Deseed and slice pepper. Put cooled lentils, bacon, onion and pepper into the dish with the dressing and mix well.

Cut tomatoes into wedges. Shell eggs and cut into wedges. Slice frankfurters. Arrange on top of lentil salad and sprinkle with parsley or chives. Serve with black bread.

Prawn and chicory salad

Overall timing 30 minutes plus chilling

Freezing Not suitable

To serve 4

2	Small heads of chicory	2
3 tbsp	Lemon juice	3x15 ml
4	Tomatoes	4
1	Fresh green chilli	1
8 oz	Shelled prawns	225 g
1 tbsp	White wine vinegar	15 ml
	Salt and pepper	
4 oz	Cream cheese	125 g
3 tbsp	Plain yogurt	3x15 ml
1	Garlic clove	1
$\frac{1}{4}$ teasp	Powdered mustard	1.25 ml
2 tbsp	Oil	2x15 ml

Remove any wilted outside leaves from the chicory, cut off the bases and scoop out the cores. Cut across into $\frac{1}{2}$ inch (12.5 mm) thick slices. Put into a bowl, add 2 tbsp (2x15 ml) of the lemon juice and toss.

Blanch, peel and quarter the tomatoes. Deseed and thinly slice the chilli. Put into a salad bowl with the tomatoes, prawns, vinegar and seasoning. Add the chicory and toss together lightly.

Put the cheese and yogurt into a bowl and beat till smooth. Add the peeled and crushed garlic, mustard, oil and remaining lemon juice. Season to taste and trickle over the salad. Chill for 15 minutes.

Just before serving, toss salad lightly till ingredients are evenly coated.

Asparagus and potato salad

Overall timing 25 minutes plus chilling

Freezing Not suitable

To serve 4

1 lb	New potatoes	450 g
	Salt and pepper	
1	Small onion	1
1 tbsp	Lemon juice	15 ml
¼ pint	Thick mayonnaise	150 ml
12 oz	Can of asparagus spears or tips	340 g
1	Hard-boiled egg	1
4	Anchovy fillets	4
2 teasp	Drained capers	2x5 ml

Scrape the potatoes and cut into even-sized chunks. Cook in boiling salted water for about 5 minutes till tender. Drain and place in a large bowl.

Peel the onion and chop finely. Stir gently into the potatoes with the lemon juice and plenty of seasoning. Add the mayonnaise and mix well.

Drain the asparagus (if using spears, cut into 2 inch/5 cm lengths), and fold gently into the salad. Arrange in a serving dish.

Shell the hard-boiled egg and cut into quarters lengthways. Arrange round the dish. Arrange anchovy fillets in a cross on the salad. Garnish with capers and chill for 30 minutes before serving with wholemeal or black bread.

Index